The LLC and Corporation Start-Up Guide

The LLC and Corporation Start-Up Guide

Mark Warda

Attorney at Law

SPHINX® PUBLISHING

AN IMPRINT OF SOURCEBOOKS, INC.®
NAPERVILLE, ILLINOIS
www.SphinxLegal.com

First Edition: 2007

Published by: Sphinx® Publishing, An Imprint of Sourcebooks, Inc.®

Naperville Office
P.O. Box 4410
Naperville, Illinois 60567-4410
630-961-3900
Fax: 630-961-2168
www.sourcebooks.com
www.SphinxLegal.com

This publication is designed to provide accurate and authoritative information in regard to the subject matter covered. It is sold with the understanding that the publisher is not engaged in rendering legal, accounting, or other professional service. If legal advice or other expert assistance is required, the services of a competent professional person should be sought.

From a Declaration of Principles Jointly Adopted by a Committee of the
American Bar Association and a Committee of Publishers and Associations

This product is not a substitute for legal advice.

Disclaimer required by Texas statutes.

Library of Congress Cataloging-in-Publication Data
Warda, Mark.
   The LLC and corporation start-up guide / by Mark Warda. -- 1st ed.
      p. cm.
   Includes index.
   ISBN-13: 978-1-57248-611-9 (pbk. : alk. paper)
   ISBN-10: 1-57248-611-2 (pbk. : alk. paper)
   1. Corporation law--United States--Popular works. 2. Private companies--United States--Popular works. I. Title.

KF1414.6.W37 2007
346.73'066--dc22
                                                            2007019323

Printed and bound in the United States of America.

Contents

Section I: **Limited Liability Companies**

Section II: **Corporations**

Using Self-Help Law Books

Before using a self-help law book, you should realize the advantages and disadvantages of doing your own legal work and understand the challenges and diligence that this requires.

The Growing Trend

Rest assured that you will not be the first or only person handling your own legal matter. For example, in some states, more than 75% of the people in divorces and other cases represent themselves. Because of the high cost of legal services, this is a major trend, and many courts are struggling to make it easier for people to represent themselves. However, some courts are not happy with people who do not use attorneys and refuse to help them in any way. For some, the attitude is, "Go to the law library and figure it out for yourself."

We write and publish self-help law books to give people an alternative to the often complicated and confusing legal books found in most law libraries. We have made the explanations of the law as simple and easy to understand as possible. Of course, unlike an attorney advising an individual client, we cannot cover every conceivable possibility.

Cost/Value Analysis

Whenever you shop for a product or service, you are faced with various levels of quality and price. In deciding what product or service to buy, you make a cost/value analysis on the basis of your willingness to pay and the quality you desire.

When buying a car, you decide whether you want transportation, comfort, status, or sex appeal. Accordingly, you decide among choices such as a Neon, a Lincoln, a Rolls Royce, or a Porsche. Before making a decision, you usually weigh the merits of each option against the cost.

When you get a headache, you can take a pain reliever (such as aspirin) or visit a medical specialist for a neurological examination. Given this choice, most people, of course, take a pain reliever, since it costs only pennies; whereas a medical examination costs hundreds of dollars and takes a lot of time. This is usually a logical choice because it is rare to need anything more than a pain reliever for a headache. But in some cases, a headache may indicate a brain tumor, and failing to see a specialist right away can result in complications. Should everyone with a headache go to a specialist? Of course not, but people treating their own illnesses must realize that they are betting, on the basis of their cost/value analysis of the situation, that they are taking the most logical option.

The same cost/value analysis must be made when deciding to do one's own legal work. Many legal situations are very straightforward, requiring a simple form and no complicated analysis. Anyone with a little intelligence and a book of instructions can handle the matter without outside help.

But there is always the chance that complications are involved that only an attorney would notice. To simplify the law into a book like this, several legal cases often must be condensed into a single sentence or paragraph. Otherwise, the book would be several hundred pages long and too complicated for most people. However, this simplification necessarily leaves out many details and nuances that would apply to special or unusual situations. Also, there are many ways to interpret most legal questions. Your case may come before a judge who disagrees with the analysis of our authors.

Therefore, in deciding to use a self-help law book and to do your own legal work, you must realize that you are making a cost/value analysis. You have decided that the money you will save in doing it yourself outweighs the chance that your case will not turn out to your satisfaction. Most people handling their own simple legal matters never have a problem, but occasionally people find that it ended up costing them more to have an attorney straighten out the situation than it would have if they had hired an attorney in the beginning. Keep this in mind while handling your case, and be sure to consult an attorney if you feel you might need further guidance.

Local Rules

The next thing to remember is that a book which covers the law for the entire nation, or even for an entire state, cannot possibly include every procedural difference of every jurisdiction. Whenever possible, we provide the exact form needed; however, in some areas, each county, or even each judge, may require unique forms and procedures. In our state books, our

forms usually cover the majority of counties in the state or provide exam-
ples of the type of form that will be required. In our national books, our
forms are sometimes even more general in nature but are designed to give
a good idea of the type of form that will be needed in most locations.
Nonetheless, keep in mind that your state, county, or judge may have a
requirement, or use a form, that is not included in this book.

You should not necessarily expect to be able to get all of the information
and resources you need solely from within the pages of this book. This book
will serve as your guide, giving you specific information whenever possible
and helping you to find out what else you will need to know. This is just like
if you decided to build your own backyard deck. You might purchase a book
on how to build decks. However, such a book would not include the
building codes and permit requirements of every city, town, county, and
township in the nation; nor would it include the lumber, nails, saws,
hammers, and other materials and tools you would need to actually build
the deck. You would use the book as your guide, and then do some work
and research involving such matters as whether you need a permit of some
kind, what type and grade of wood is available in your area, whether to use
hand tools or power tools, and how to use those tools.

Before using the forms in a book like this, you should check with your
court clerk to see if there are any local rules of which you should be aware
or local forms you will need to use. Often, such forms will require the same
information as the forms in the book but are merely laid out differently or
use slightly different language. They will sometimes require additional
information.

Changes in the Law

Besides being subject to local rules and practices, the law is subject to
change at any time. The courts and the legislatures of all fifty states are
constantly revising the laws. It is possible that while you are reading this
book, some aspect of the law is being changed.

In most cases, the change will be of minimal significance. A form will be
redesigned, additional information will be required, or a waiting period will
be extended. As a result, you might need to revise a form, file an extra form,
or wait out a longer time period. These types of changes will not usually

affect the outcome of your case. On the other hand, sometimes a major part of the law is changed, the entire law in a particular area is rewritten, or a case that was the basis of a central legal point is overruled. In such instances, your entire ability to pursue your case may be impaired.

Introduction

Each year millions of new businesses are registered throughout the country. For years *corporations* have been the preferred form of business, but the *limited liability company* is becoming more popular each year. The reason for this is that limited liability companies provide more flexibility and less paperwork than corporations, while offering nearly identical benefits.

The main reason people incorporate or form limited liability companies is to avoid personal liability for business debts and liabilities. While sole proprietors and partners are at risk of losing nearly everything they own, entrepreneurs who form an LLC or corporation risk only the *capital* they put up to start the venture.

Creating a basic limited liability company is not difficult. Creating a simple corporation is also very easy. It is the purpose of this book to explain, in simple language, how you can do it yourself.

Section I:

Limited Liability Companies

Chapter

What a Limited Liability Company Is

A *limited liability company* (LLC) is a relatively recent invention. For hundreds of years, the three choices for a business entity were *sole proprietorship*, *partnership*, or *corporation*. However, in 1977, the LLC was invented by the state of Wyoming to fill a new need—businesses that wanted to be taxed and managed like partnerships but protected from liability like corporations. Once the Internal Revenue Service (IRS) accepted this arrangement, every state in the union followed suit and passed laws allowing LLCs.

The laws, however, were not identical and the effectiveness of the LLCs varied from state to state. In the beginning, single-person businesses could not use them because the law stated that a sole person could not be taxed as a partnership. However, the IRS later changed the rules to allow single-person LLCs to pass through their income to the owner.

Because the early tax laws required two or more members to avoid corporate taxation, many state laws required two persons to start an LLC. However, after the tax law change, all fifty states now allow one-member LLCs.

QUICK Tip

All fifty states now allow one-member LLCs.

In some states there are disadvantages to using LLCs, because the filing fees or annual fees are higher than for other types of businesses, such as an *S corporation*. Before forming your own LLC, you should compare the fees and requirements to be sure it offers your business the most advantages.

Legally, an LLC is a legal *person*, like a corporation, that is created under state law. As a person, an LLC has certain rights and obligations, such as the right to do business and the obligation to pay taxes. (Sometimes one hears of a law referring to *natural persons*. That is to differentiate actual people from corporations and LLCs, which are considered persons, but not natural persons.)

The idea behind both the LLC and the corporation is to allow people to invest in a new business but not risk unlimited personal liability.

Common Terms

Before forming an LLC, you should be familiar with the common terms that will be used in the text.

Member

A *member* is a person who owns an interest in a limited liability company, similar to the stockholder of a corporation. In an LLC, the members have the option of running the company themselves or having managers who are or are not members. Until recently, some states required an LLC to have two or more members, but now that the IRS allows favorable tax treatment for one-member LLCs, the states are changing their laws to allow them.

Manager

A *manager* is someone who runs the affairs of an LLC. In most states, an LLC can be either managed by all the members equally, or it can have a manager or managers who may or may not be members.

Managing Member

A *managing member* is a member of the LLC who runs the operations. If all of the members do not want to manage the LLC, then one or more of them can be designated managing member.

Registered Agent and Registered Office

The *registered agent* is the person designated by a limited liability company to receive legal papers that must be served on the company. (In a few states the term *statutory agent* is used.) The registered agent should be regularly available at the registered office of the corporation. The *registered office* can be the company offices or the office of the company's attorney, or whomever is the registered agent. At the time of registration, some states require the company to file a Certificate of Designation of Registered Agent/Registered Office. This contains a statement that must be signed by the registered agent that he or she understands the duties and responsibilities of the position.

Articles of Organization

The *articles of organization* is the document that is filed to start the limited liability company. (In a few states, it may have a slightly different name, such as *certificate of organization*.) In most cases it only needs to contain a few basic statements. More provisions can be added, but usually it is better to put such provisions in the membership agreement rather than the articles, because amendment of the latter is more complicated.

Operating Agreement

The *operating agreement* is the document that sets out rights and obligations of the members and the rules for running the company. An operating agreement is not required in every state, but having one is a good idea. If such an agreement has not been signed by the members, the rules provided in your state's statute apply.

Membership Operating Agreement If the LLC is run by its members, the agreement is usually called a *membership operating agreement*. Even if the LLC has only one member, it is important to have an operating agreement to spell out the non-liability of the member for debts of the company.

Management Operating Agreement If the LLC is to be managed by less than all the members, or by someone who is not a member, there should be a management agreement spelling out the rights and duties of the members and the managers. This can be combined into the operating agreement, in which case it would be called a *management operating agreement*.

Annual Report

Most states require some sort of annual report to keep the state updated on the members and status of the company. In most cases, the company will be dissolved if this form is not filed on time, and in some states, there is a very high fee to reinstate the company.

Figure 1.1: **LLC Terms Compared with Corporations**

You may be more familiar with the terminology associated with corporations. While an LLC has distinct terms (which have specialized meaning), the following list provides a basic comparison of LLC terms with those relating to a corporation.

LLC	**Corporation**
Member	Shareholder
Manager	Director/Officer
Managing Member	Shareholder who is also a Director or Officer
Registered Agent and Registered Office	Registered Agent and Registered Office
Articles of Organization	Articles of Incorporation
Operating Agreement	Bylaws
Annual Report	Annual Report

Chapter

Advantages and Disadvantages of an LLC

Before forming a limited liability company (LLC), the business owner or prospective business owner should become familiar with the advantages and disadvantages of the LLC and how they compare to those of other business entities.

Compared to Proprietorships and Partnerships

The limited liability company offers the greatest benefits when compared to *partnerships* and *sole proprietorships*. Now that the LLC structure is available, it is advisable for most partnerships and sole proprietorships to switch.

Advantages

There are several advantages to having your business be an LLC as opposed to a partnership or sole proprietorship. This section describes some of those advantages and how to apply them to certain situations.

Limited Liability The main reason for forming a limited liability company or corporation is to limit the liability of the owners. In a sole proprietorship or partnership, the owners are personally liable for the debts and liabilities of the business, and creditors can go after nearly all of their assets to collect. If an LLC is formed and operated properly, the owners can be protected from all such liability.

EXAMPLE 1: If several people are in a partnership and one of them makes many large, extravagant purchases in the name of the partnership, the other partners can be liable for the full amount of all such purchases. The creditors can take the bank accounts, cars, real estate, and other property of any partner to pay the debts of the partnership. If only one partner has money, he or she may have to pay all of the debts accumulated by the other partners. When doing business in the LLC or corporate form, the business may go bankrupt and the shareholders may lose their initial investment, but the creditors cannot touch the personal assets of the owners.

When doing business in the LLC or corporate form, the business may go bankrupt and the shareholders may lose their initial investment, but the creditors cannot touch the personal assets of the owners.

EXAMPLE 2: If an employee of a partnership causes a terrible accident, the partnership and all the partners can be held personally liable for millions of dollars in damages. With a corporation or LLC, only the business would be liable whether or not there was enough money to cover the damages.

QUICK Tip

If a member of a limited liability company does something negligent, signs a debt personally, or guarantees a company debt, the limited liability company will not protect him or her from the consequences of his or her own act or from the debt. Also, if a limited liability company fails to follow proper formalities, a court may use that as an excuse to hold the members liable. The formalities include having separate bank accounts, filing annual reports, and following other requirements of state law.

Since the limited liability company is relatively new, there have been few cases interpreting the law. Courts will most likely look to both corporation and partnership law when ruling in a limited liability company case. When a court ignores a corporate structure and holds the owners or officers liable, it is called *piercing the corporate veil*. (It is not yet clear how or when the courts would allow a party to pierce the LLC structure.)

Continuous Existence A limited liability company may have a perpetual existence. When a sole proprietor dies, the assets of his or her business may pass to the heirs, but the business no longer exists. (This may also happen with a partnership if it is not set up properly.) If the surviving spouse or other heirs of a business owner want to continue the business in their own names, they will be considered a new business—even if they are using the assets of the old business. With a partnership, the death of one partner can cause a dissolution of the business if there is no provision in the partnership agreement for it to continue.

EXAMPLE: If the owner of a sole proprietorship dies, his or her spouse may want to continue the business. That person may inherit all of the assets, but would have to start a new business. This means getting new licenses and tax numbers, registering the name, and establishing credit from scratch. With an LLC, the business continues with all of the same licenses, bank accounts, and so on.

Ease of Transferability A limited liability company and all of its assets and accounts may be transferred by the simple transfer of interest in the company. With a sole proprietorship, each of the individual assets must be transferred and the accounts, licenses, and permits must be individually transferred.

EXAMPLE: If a sole proprietorship is sold, the new owner will have to get a new occupational license, set up his or her own bank account, and apply for a new taxpayer identification number. The title to any vehicles or real estate will have to be put in the new owner's name, and all open accounts will have to be changed to his or her name. He or she will probably have to submit new credit applications. With an LLC, all of these items remain in the same business name and are under control of the new manager or officer.

Sharing Ownership With a limited liability company, the owner of a business can share the profits of a business without giving up control. This is done by setting up the share of profits separate from the share of ownership.

EXAMPLE: John wants to give his children some of the profits of his business. He can make them members of the company entitled to a share of the profits without giving them any control over the management. This would not be practical with a partnership or sole proprietorship.

When switching taxpayer identification numbers, the new owners will have to submit personal applications for such things as credit lines or liquor licenses.

Ease of Raising Capital A limited liability company may raise capital by admitting new members or borrowing money. In most cases, a business does not pay taxes on money it raises through the sale of its shares.

EXAMPLE: If an LLC wants to expand, the owners can sell 10%, 50%, or 90% of the ownership and still remain in control of the business. The people putting up the money may be more willing to invest if they know they will have a piece of the action than if they were making a loan with a limited return. They may not want to become partners in a partnership.

Alert!

There are strict rules about selling interests in businesses, with criminal penalties and triple damages for violators.

Figure 2.1: **Advantages of an LLC**

▶ **SEPARATE RECORDKEEPING**

An LLC has all its own bank accounts and records. A sole proprietor may have trouble differentiating which expenses were for business and which were for personal items.

▶ **EASE OF ESTATE PLANNING**

With an LLC or corporation, shares of a company can be distributed more easily than with a partnership or sole proprietorship. Different heirs can be given different percentages, and control can be limited to those who are most capable.

▶ **PRESTIGE**

The name of an LLC can sound more prestigious than the name of a sole proprietor. John Smith d/b/a Acme Builders sounds like one lone guy. Acme Builders, LLC, sounds like it might be a large, sophisticated operation. One female writer on the subject has suggested that a woman who is president of a corporation looks more successful than a woman doing business in her own name. This would be the same with an LLC and would apply to everyone.

▶ **SEPARATE CREDIT RATING**

An LLC has its own credit rating, which can be better or worse than the owner's credit rating. An LLC can go bankrupt while the owner's credit remains unaffected, or an owner's credit may be bad, but the LLC may maintain a good rating.

Disadvantages

The main disadvantage that most professionals see in the LLC is that the law is new and it is not yet known how the courts will interpret it. (For some lawyers, this is an excuse not to learn new things.) It is always more comfortable to do what you have always done. However, while there is always a chance for bad interpretation of the law, most cases should turn out as the law intended, and owners of LLCs should be protected from liability.

Cost Compared to a sole proprietorship or partnership, an LLC is more expensive to operate. In some states the fees are as low as $50 or even $10, but in others they are hundreds of dollars each year. However, this cost is offset by the lesser need for liability insurance.

Separate Records The owners of a limited liability company must be careful to keep their personal business separate from the business of the limited liability company. The LLC must have its own records and should have minutes of meetings. Money must be kept separate. Records should be separate in every business and the structure of a company might make it easier to do so.

Taxes A limited liability company owner will have to pay unemployment compensation tax for him- or herself, which he or she would not have to pay as a sole proprietor—unless he or she opts to be taxed as an S corporation.

A 2007 court decision held that if an LLC opts to be taxed as a partnership or proprietorship, the owner could be personally liable for unpaid payroll taxes.

Banking Checks made out to an LLC cannot be cashed; they must be deposited into a corporate account. Some banks have higher fees just for such accounts.

Compared to Limited Partnerships

A *limited partnership* is an entity in which one or more partners control the business and are liable for the debts (the *general partners*), and one or more partners have no say in the business nor liability for the debts (the *limited partners*). This is expensive to set up because the limited partnership agreement is costly.

The limited liability company allows a similar structure at a lower cost with the added benefit that no one needs to be liable for the debts of the business. For most businesses that were once limited partnerships, the LLC is now the preferred form of business.

Compared to Corporations

The biggest advantage of an LLC over a corporation is that in most states it provides *double asset protection*. A corporation provides asset protection in that a shareholder is protected from liabilities of the corporation, but a member of an LLC gets this protection, plus personal creditors cannot take his or her LLC away from him or her if it is set up correctly.

Double Asset Protection

The really great thing about the LLC is that it offers two types of asset protection. One is the same as a corporation; the other is the same as a limited partnership. Together these make the LLC one of the most valuable asset protection tools that exist.

Corporate-Type Protection A corporation protects its owners from liability in that the shareholders are protected from the debts and liabilities of the business. If you own stock in General Motors, you will not be liable if they default on their bonds or if someone sues General Motors for defective cars and wins billions of dollars.

This same type of protection is available to you if you own a corporation (S corporation or C corporation) or an LLC. If the company is liable for something (and you did not personally cause it), then you as the shareholder or member will in most cases not be liable.

Limited Partnership-Type Protection In most states an LLC provides an additional type of asset protection—protection of your LLC interest from your personal creditors. This means that if you do something personally that makes you liable—for example, you get into an auto accident—the creditor cannot take your LLC assets away from you. What the law says is that your creditor can only get a *charging order* against your interest. This means that it has to pay taxes on the income of the LLC, but that it cannot get any money out of the LLC unless the other LLC members decide to give it. Needless to say, most creditors do not even want charging orders.

Any assets you put into an LLC can be safe from your personal creditors, no matter what you do—malpractice, auto accidents, divorce, bankruptcy, etc. However, note the word *can*. In law, nothing is black and white, and new law is an especially gray area. If you follow the rules, however, you can be successful.

Requirements for Double Asset Protection While the law says that a creditor can only have a charging order against an LLC interest, at least one court has ruled that if the LLC has only one member, the creditor can take the company. The rationale was that the charging order rule was designed to protect other members of a business from disruption from one member's creditors, and this does not make sense in a one-member company. So you need at least two members of your LLC to get the double asset protection.

QUICK Tip

You need at least two members of your LLC to get the double asset protection.

Entrepreneurs who do not really want someone else in their business look for ways to have a two-member company, but to still keep full control. Some of the suggestions have been to have part of the LLC owned by:

- a corporation owned by the member;
- another LLC owned by the member;
- a trust owned by the member;
- a trust set up for a child or children;
- a child; or,
- a parent.

Will these work? If the one member really controls 100%, then probably not. Courts usually look to the substance of the whole transaction to see what the reality is. If you just assign 2% of your LLC to your corporation solely to avoid creditors, it will probably be considered a sham transaction.

What would work would be a setup with some purpose. If your parent made a small investment in your business in exchange for a small percentage of ownership, that would be legitimate. If you set up a trust for your children's education, and it bought a part of your LLC, that would probably also be seen as legitimate.

> **EXAMPLE:** One doctor sold a small percentage of his LLC to his accountant. If this appeared to be a plan to share profits in exchange for services, rather than merely a sham, it might work.

One thing to consider is that the success of a plan depends on the sophistication of the creditor. A thorough examination by a sophisticated creditor's attorney could make any plan look suspect; however, if a new attorney is faced with multiple LLCs and a complicated setup that could take months to decipher, he or she might be willing to accept your settlement offer or insurance limits rather than spend the time to try to get through it.

The fact that this is a gray area of law works two ways. For the person wanting the protection, it does not give clear answers on what works best, but for the creditor, it does not provide how to win. No matter what type of LLC arrangement you have set up, if a creditor wins against you, you can appeal it and argue that the law gives you more protection. Lawyers do not like to spend years in court unless there is a significant payoff. A small business with a complicated structure and no sure legal basis would be a good candidate for a quick settlement.

Figure 2.2: **Other Advantages of an LLC over a Corporation**

▶ An LLC requires less formality than a corporation. While improper procedures in a corporation may allow a creditor to pierce the corporate veil and hold shareholders liable, the LLC is meant to be a safe harbor to protect business owners from liability.

▶ An LLC can make special allocations of profits and losses among members, whereas an S corporation cannot. S corporations must have one class of ownership in which profits and losses are allocated according to the percentage of ownership.

▶ In an LLC, money borrowed by the company can increase the tax basis of the owners (and lower the taxes); whereas in an S corporation, it does not.

▶ Contributing property to set up an LLC is not taxable even for minority interest owners. In the case of a corporation, the Internal Revenue Code Section 351 only allows it to be tax-free for the contributors who have control of the business.

▶ The owners of an LLC can be foreign persons, other corporations, or any kind of trust. This is not true for the owners of S corporations.

▶ An LLC may have an unlimited number of members while an S corporation is limited to one hundred.

▶ If an S corporation violates one of the rules, it can lose its S corporation status and not be allowed to regain it for five years.

 Another advantage may be psychological. The LLC is still a relatively new entity, and in the twenty-first century it may look more up-to-date to be an LLC rather than an ordinary corporation.

Disadvantage

The main disadvantage of an LLC, which is taxed as a disregarded entity compared to an S corporation, is that with an S corporation, profits taken out other than salary are not subject to Social Security and Medicare taxes (15.3% at the time of publication); whereas all profits of an LLC are subject to these taxes (up to the taxable limits). However, if this is an issue for you, you can opt to have your LLC taxed as a corporation and then choose S corporation status.

For a large business where the owners take out salaries of $80,000 or more plus profits, there would not be much difference since the Social Security tax does not apply above that level. However, for a smaller business where an owner would take out, say, $30,000 salary and $20,000 profit, the extra taxes would be over $3,000.

In some states, the start-up and annual fees for an LLC are higher than for an S corporation.

When to Use a Single-Member Company

While a single-member LLC does not provide double asset protection, it can still be very useful in many situations. Remember, a single-member LLC protects the owner against business claims but does not protect the business from the member's creditors. So the best use occurs when the business would have claims, but the company does not have many assets worth claiming.

A good example is a property management company. Many real estate investors have one LLC set up to manage their properties. Usually it will collect the rents and pay the mortgages and expenses of the properties. This company deals with the tenants and has a high risk of getting sued. However, if it spends all the money it collects in rents, it will not have many assets so it does not need double asset protection.

Another use could be to own individual properties. If you have one LLC that owns five properties, then a liability on one of them could cause you to lose them all. A better plan would be to have each property in a separate single-member LLC all owned by one multiple-member LLC. The single-member LLCs would not file tax returns but would pass through their income to the multiple-member LLC. *(Thanks to David Burton, CPA, of Harper Van Skoik & Co., Clearwater, FL, for this planning.)*

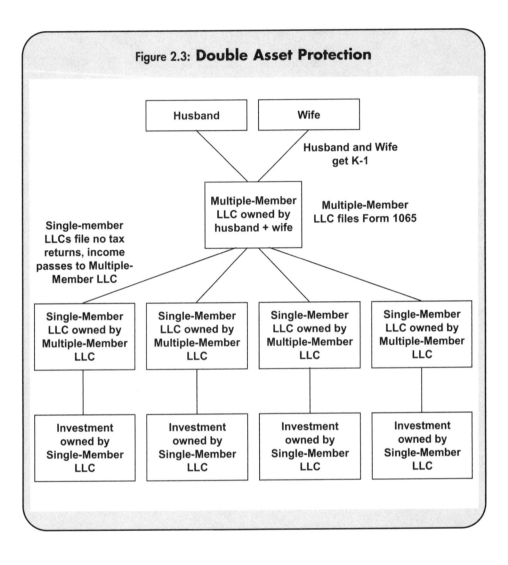

Figure 2.3: **Double Asset Protection**

Figure 2.4: **Business Comparison Chart**

	Sole Partnership	General Partnership	Limited Partnership	Limited Liability Co.	Corporation C or S	Nonprofit Corporation
Liability Protection	No	No	For limited partners	For all members	For all shareholders	For all members
Taxes	Pass through	Pass through	Pass through	Pass through or LLC can pay	S corps. pass through C corps. pay tax	None on income— Employees pay on wages
Minimum # of Members	1	2	2	1	1	1 to 3
Diff. Classes of Ownership	No	Yes	Yes	Yes	S corps.–No C corps.–Yes	No ownership— Different classes of membership
Survives after Death	No	No	Yes	Yes	Yes	Yes
Best for	1 person, low-risk business or no assets	Low-risk business	Low-risk business with silent partners	All types of businesses	All types of businesses	Educational

Converting an Existing Business

While an LLC may appear to be the best type of business entity for you, if you have an existing business, you should weigh the time and expense involved in making the conversion.

A sole proprietorship would be the easiest to convert, and a corporation would be the most complicated. (The corporation has potential tax issues which should be reviewed by a tax specialist.) At a minimum, some of the things which will have to be handled in your conversion are federal employer identification number, state tax account numbers, fictitious name registration, business licenses, professional licenses (if any), bank accounts, vendor accounts, customer accounts, and utilities.

Chapter

Types of LLCs

Before forming your limited liability company, you need to decide which type of LLC it will be. There are several choices to choose from, each based on your particular circumstance.

Domestic LLC or Foreign LLC

A person wishing to form a limited liability company must decide whether the company will be a *domestic* LLC or a *foreign* LLC. For the purposes of this book, a domestic LLC is one you form in the state in which you do business, and a foreign LLC is one you form in another state to do business in your state.

Delaware LLCs

In the past, there was an advantage to forming a business in Delaware, because of its liberal business laws and a long history of court decisions favorable to businesses. Many national corporations were formed there for that reason. However, most states have liberalized their business laws over the years. Today, in most cases, there is no advantage to forming a business in Delaware unless you are doing business there.

However, it would be an advantage to form an LLC in Delaware if you live in a state with high LLC fees or a high personal income tax. If the sole purpose of your LLC was to own a piece of property (as opposed to running a business), you could take advantage of Delaware's lower fees. Be sure to check your state's definition of doing business to make sure your activities are outside of it; otherwise, you will end up paying double fees—your state's full fees plus Delaware's.

To save on income taxes, you could form a Delaware company that would siphon profits away from your local company—for example, by providing consulting services out of state. The money paid would avoid your state income tax and Delaware does not have an income tax on LLCs. (You would not avoid federal income taxes, only your state's income tax.)

Nevada LLCs

Nevada has liberalized its business laws recently to attract more companies. It allows more privacy and other benefits depending on the type of entity. It does not have a state income tax, nor does it share information with the Internal Revenue Service. If your state has high LLC fees or a state income tax, the benefits described for a Delaware LLC would also apply to Nevada.

QUICK Tip

If privacy is your main concern, you should do more research on what organizing in Nevada could do for you.

Disadvantage

The biggest disadvantage to forming a business in Nevada, Delaware, or any state other than the one you are in, is you will need to have an agent or an office in that state and will have to register as a foreign corporation doing business in your state. This is more expensive and more complicated than registering in your own state. You can also be sued in the state in which your company was formed. This would be more expensive for you to defend than a suit filed in your local court. Additionally, if you incorporate in a state that has an income tax, you may have to pay taxes there even if you only do business in your own state.

Membership Controlled or Management Controlled

The next thing you will need to decide is whether your LLC will be membership controlled or management controlled. If the LLC is being formed by one person or a small group of people who will all operate it as partners, you should designate it as membership controlled and execute a *membership operating agreement*. If the LLC will have silent partners and be managed by other members or nonmembers, you should designate it management controlled and execute a *management operating agreement*.

LLC or PLLC

In many states, professionals such as lawyers, doctors, veterinarians, architects, life insurance agents, chiropractors, and accountants are allowed to set up LLCs. These are designated *professional service limited liability companies* (PLLCs) or something of a similar nature.

Again, since the laws covering professional LLCs are state laws, you will need to get a copy of your state's statute to be sure your plan complies with all of the requirements. You should also check with the *licensing board* that regulates your profession to see if it imposes any additional requirements on professional LLCs. In some states, professionals may be required to obtain malpractice insurance if they form a PLLC.

**Figure 3.1: Additional Rules that May Apply
to Professional LLCs**

▶ The professional limited liability company must have one specific purpose spelled out in the articles of organization, and the purpose must be to practice one of the professions. Usually the PLLC may not engage in any other business, but it may invest its funds in real estate, stocks, bonds, mortgages, or other types of investments.

▶ The name of the professional service LLC must contain the word "chartered" or "professional limited company" or the abbreviation "PLLC."

▶ Only persons licensed to practice the profession may be members of a professional service limited liability company, and a member who loses his or her right to practice must immediately sever all employment with and financial interests in the company.

▶ A professional service limited liability company may not merge with any other limited liability company except another professional service corporation that is licensed to perform the same type of services.

Single-Member or Multiple-Member

Whether you use a single-member or multiple-member LLC is not just a function of the number of people involved. Because of the advantages and disadvantages of each, a single business owner might want to form a multiple-member company and multiple people might want to form single-member companies.

For example, a person with a one-person business who wants to start a multiple-member LLC to gain asset protection might want to make his or her spouse, parent, or child a member. Two people who own lots of properties as separate LLCs might want to make them single-member LLCs owned by one multiple-member LLC to avoid filing a separate tax return for each.

You will have an operating agreement whether you are a single- or multiple-member company. However, for a multiple-member company, you need to be more careful to spell out each others' rights in the event of a split-up, death, or irreconcilable disagreement.

Taxes

A single-member LLC is easier for tax purposes because no tax return is required. The income is reported on the member's tax return. A multiple-member LLC must file IRS Form 1065, file the partnership tax return, and give the members K-1 forms to file with their returns. If you do your own taxes, this may be just another form to file, but if you have a professional tax preparer, it may cost hundreds of dollars. If you set up numerous LLCs, this can get expensive.

Asset Protection

While a single-member LLC is simpler for tax purposes, it probably will not be allowed double asset protection. You need two or more members for the double asset protection that an LLC offers. Therefore, if your LLC will have substantial assets, it should be set up as multiple-member to obtain double asset protection.

Chapter  4

Start-Up Procedures

This chapter explains the steps you need to follow in setting up your LLC.

Choosing the Company Name

The very first thing to do before starting a limited liability company is to thoroughly research the name you wish to use, to be sure it is available. Many businesses have been forced to stop using their name after spending thousands of dollars promoting it because another business was already using it.

Local Records

To check for other businesses in your state using a certain name, you can call or write your secretary of state's office, or in some states, you can do your own search using their website. The phone number, address, and website address for your state (if applicable) is in Appendix A. If your name is too similar to another company's name, you will not be allowed to register it.

You should also ask about *fictitious* or *assumed names*. In some states, these are registered with the secretary of state, and in others, with the county recorder or court office. In some states, the secretary of state does not limit the number of people who may register the same name. Instead, an infringement would depend upon whether they used the name in the same area.

Business Listings

Since some businesses neglect to properly register their name (yet still may have superior rights to the name), you should also check phone books and business directories. Many libraries have phone books from around the country, as well as directories of trade names.

Federal Trademarks

It is possible to use a name similar to the names of businesses elsewhere in the country without problems, but if they have registered a federal trademark of the name, they can force you to stop using it, and you could be liable for damages. It is best to check the trademarks registered with the United States Patent and Trademark Office (PTO).

The PTO records are not completely up-to-date, and without experience at searching them you might miss a trademark. You might want to hire a professional search company to give you a written report. Some firms that do searches include the following.

Government Liaison Services, Inc.
200 North Glebe Road, Suite 321
Arlington, VA 22203
800-642-6564
www.trademarkinfo.com

Thomson & Thomson
500 Victory Road
North Quincy, MA 02171
800-692-8833
www.thomson-thomson.com

XL Corporate Service
62 White Street
New York, NY 10013
212-431-5000

Figure 4.1: **Trademark Records Search**

Up until 1999, the only ways to search the records of the United States Patent and Trademark Office were to go there, use a Trademark Depository Library, or hire a search firm to do a search. Now you can do a search instantly on the Internet. The website is www.uspto.gov. Once there, click on "Search" under "Trademarks" on the left side of the screen. Here is what you will see:

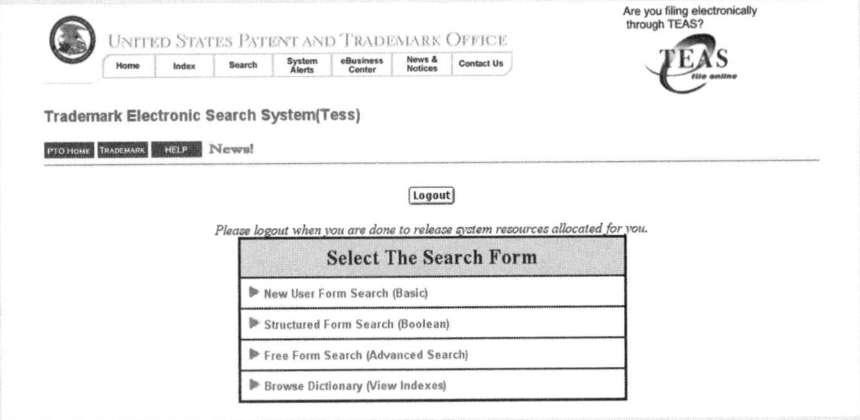

The database is updated regularly, but it is usually a few weeks behind schedule. You will see the date it is current through in the first paragraph. Clicking on the "News!" button will give you the latest complete filing date available online from the PTO. As a practical matter, if a mark you are considering has not been registered in the last two hundred years, it is not likely that it has been in the last few weeks, but it is possible, especially if you are using a mark related to the latest technology. If you wish to update your mark through the latest filings, you will need to either visit the PTO or hire a search firm to do so.

Similar Names

Sometimes it seems like every good name is taken, but a name can often be modified slightly or used for a different type of goods or services. If there is a "TriCounty Painting, L.L.C." in another part of your state, it may be possible to use something such as "TriCounty Painting of Libertyville, L.L.C." if you are in a different part of the state. Try different variations if your favorite is taken. Keep in mind that if you eventually expand your business to an area where the name is being used, you can be barred from using it in that area. In such a case, you would be better off using a completely different name.

Another possibility is to give the LLC one name and do business under a fictitious name. (See "Fictitious or Assumed Names" on page 37.)

EXAMPLE: If you want to use the name "Flowers by Freida" in your city and there is already a "Flowers by Freida, Inc." in another part of the state, you might register your company under the name "Freida Jones, L.L.C." and register the company as doing business under the fictitious name "Flowers by Freida." Unless "Flowers by Freida, Inc." has registered a state or federal trademark for the name, you will probably be able to use the name.

You should realize that you might run into complications later, especially if you decide to expand into other areas of the state. One protection available would be to register the name as a trademark. This would give you exclusive use of the name anywhere that someone else was not already using it.

Name Requirements

There are requirements that the limited liability company name contain wording indicating that it is a limited liability company. Depending on the state, it may require one or all of the following:

L.C.	LC	limited company
L.L.C.	LLC	limited liability company

In some states you can use just the word "limited" or the abbreviation "ltd." Be sure to check your state rules before making a choice.

The name cannot include any words implying that it is part of the state or federal government or that it is in any business in which it is not authorized to be.

In some states, professional LLCs must also use certain words, such as "chartered" or "professional limited liability company." Again, the specific state rule must be checked.

Figure 4.2: **Forbidden Names**

A limited liability company may not use certain words in its name if there would be a likelihood of confusion. There are state and federal laws that control the use of these words. In most cases, your application will be rejected if you use a forbidden word. Some of the words that may not be used without special licenses or registration are:

Assurance	Insurance
Banc	Lottery
Bank	Olympiad
Banker	Olympic
Banking	Savings Bank
College	Savings and Loan Association
Cooperative	Trust Company
Credit Union	University
Disney	

Trademarks

The name of a business cannot be registered as a trademark, unless the name is used in connection with goods and services. In that case, it may be registered and such registration will grant the holder exclusive rights to use that name except in areas where someone else has already used the name. A trademark may be registered either in each state or in the United States Patent and Trademark Office (PTO), which covers the entire country.

Each trademark is registered for a certain *class* of goods. If you want to sell "Zapata" chewing gum, it does not matter that someone has registered the name "Zapata" for use in another category, such as shoes. (An exception to this rule is where a trademark has become famous. For example, even though Coca-Cola is a trademark for a beverage, you could not use the name Coca-Cola for chewing gum.) If you want to register the mark for several types of goods or services, you must register it for each different class into which the goods or services fall, and pay a separate fee for each category.

Every state has a procedure for registering a trademark for statewide protection. This protects a mark throughout the state from anyone who might want to use the same mark in the future, but does not affect the rights of people who already use the mark in the state. It also does not stop people in other states from using the mark. The form is simple and the cost is minimal in most states. For more information, phone, write, or check the website of your secretary of state.

For protection across the entire United States, the mark can be registered with the United States Patent and Trademark Office for a fee of $325 if filed online, or $375 if paper filed. The procedure for federal registration is more complicated than state registration. You can find some information and forms on the website of the PTO at **www.uspto.gov**.

Unregistered Names

Even if a business does not register its name, it still has legal rights to it. Therefore, you should check to see if any other businesses have the name you intend to use. If a business in your area has a similar name, you should not use it. If the business is farther away, you can use it if you do not expect to do business in that area, but a completely different name is still better.

For a thorough search, you can use the Internet search engines Google or Yahoo, but you may find more listings than you can ever look at. If you go to a White Pages listing of business names, you will get a more limited list. One site that lets you search all states at once is **www.switchboard.com**.

Fictitious or Assumed Names

The name of an LLC is its legal name. However, it can also operate under a *fictitious name* (called an *assumed name* in some states) just as an individual can. This is done when a company wants to operate several businesses under different names or if the business name is not available as a company name.

> **EXAMPLE:** An LLC may have the legal name Elizabeth Bartlett, LLC, and open a bakery called "Betty B's Breads & Buns."

Registration of a fictitious name is either done with the secretary of state or a county recorder. Check with the office in your area for forms and instructions.

QUICK Tip

When a fictitious name is used by a limited liability company, the company's legal name should also be used in conjunction with it whenever possible. If the public does not see that they are dealing with a limited liability company, they may be able to use the theory of piercing the corporate veil to collect against the members individually.

State LLC Laws and Forms

Each state has adopted its own version of the statute allowing LLCs, so each state will have slightly different requirements as to what the filing documents must contain. Also, not every state will supply the same materials. Some send only a single page of vague instructions, while others send a large packet including a copy of the statute and numerous forms.

If your state provides a form, using that form may speed up your proceedings. Some states provide the form in downloadable format on the Internet, and others only use the mail. (California appears to be the only state that requires its own form to be used.) Other states allow people to draft their own articles as long as all the required information is included. If your state does not provide a form, or if you wish to get started without waiting for the form, you can use the blank form in this book or retype the information yourself. The good thing about forming an LLC is that if you make a mistake, such as forgetting a required provision, the filing office will usually return it for correction rather than let you file it wrong and have a defective company.

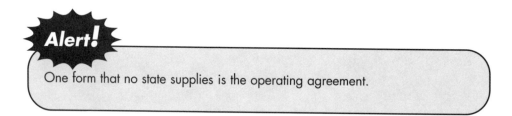

Alert!

One form that no state supplies is the operating agreement.

You can get the statutes for most states on the Internet. If you do not have access to the Internet, you may be able to obtain a copy from your secretary of state or your state legislator, or photocopy it at the library.

When getting a copy of your state statute, find out the date it was last updated and when your state legislature convenes. If a session recently ended, there may be changes to the law that are not included in your copy of the statute. A librarian at a law library would be most knowledgeable as to which copy of the statute is most up-to-date.

Once you get a copy of the laws, you should become familiar with the filing and operational requirements for LLCs. General rules are included in this book, but some states have some more specific requirements. Do not be intimidated if the statute is long. Many of the provisions will apply to *mergers* or *dissolutions*, which do not concern you at this point.

Articles of Organization

The action that creates the limited liability company in most states is the filing of *articles of organization* with the secretary of state. In a few states there may be another filing office or the document may have a slightly different name. (Some states require additional forms to complete the registration, as explained in Figure 4.3.)

Usual Requirements

Requirements for the articles of organization are listed below. Some states require an extra clause or two, and these are discussed on page 41.

Name The name must include the suffix (LLC, LC, etc.).

Purpose Many states require that the business purpose be stated, though this may be stated as "any lawful purpose for which limited liability companies may be formed." A few states ask for a specific *industry code*.

Period of Duration The period of duration may be stated as perpetual in most states. In Utah, it cannot exceed ninety-nine years, and in Nebraska and South Dakota, it cannot exceed thirty years.

Name and Street Address of the Initial Registered (or Statutory) Agent In many states, the registered agent also must sign a form stating that he or she is familiar with and accepts the obligations of the position.

Each limited liability company must have a *registered agent* and a *registered office*. The registered agent can be any individual or a corporation. The registered office can be the business office of the limited liability company if the registered agent works out of that office, or it can be the office of another individual who is the registered agent (such as an attorney) or a corporate registered agent's office. The business address of the registered agent is considered the registered office of the limited liability company. In most LLCs, one of the members is the registered agent at the business address. Technically, it may not be a residence unless that address is also a business office of the limited liability company.

Management The management section must state whether the company will be managed by the members or by separate managers. In most states, all of their names and addresses must be included, whether or not they are members or separate managers.

Principle Place of Business The principle place of business must be a street address in most states, but a mailing address can also be included.

Effective Date Many states want to know the effective date of the articles. Usually, this is the date of filing.

Nonliability Five states (Hawaii, South Carolina, South Dakota, Vermont, and West Virginia) require a statement of whether the members are liable for the debts of the company. Several other states say that a clause can be added stating whether the members are liable. Since the main purpose of forming an LLC is to avoid personal liability, a nonliability clause is included in the articles in this book. If using a state form, you should not check any box stating that the members are liable.

It is best to keep your articles to the bare legal minimum and put any other provisions in the operating agreement. This is because it is much easier to amend the operating agreement than the articles if you want to make changes at a later date.

Additional Clauses

The following clauses are sometimes put into LLC articles of organization. In some states, one or more of these clauses may be required. (See your state page in Appendix A for "Articles of Organization Special Requirements.")

The Right, If Any, to Admit New Members If the LLC will allow new members to be admitted, there must be a clause stating so. Some states require this to be in the articles along with the terms and conditions of admission. Here is some sample language:

> New members can be admitted to the company with full rights of membership upon the unanimous consent of the existing members.

Members' Rights to Continue Business This clause states whether the remaining members can continue the business after the death, retirement, resignation, expulsion, bankruptcy, or dissolution of a member, or any other event that terminates membership. Some states require that this be spelled out. Here is a sample clause:

> The company can continue the business after the death, retirement, resignation, expulsion, bankruptcy, or dissolution of a member, or any other event that terminates membership, upon the unanimous consent of the remaining members.

Organizers In some cases, the organizers of the company are different from the members (such as if an attorney or paralegal files the papers). Colorado, the District of Columbia, Illinois, and Oregon require that the organizers be disclosed in the articles.

Professional LLCs

In most states, there is a separate portion of the statutes that governs professional LLCs and other professional companies. This contains specific requirements that these entities must follow. Some typical things that the statute may require are:

- the business purpose is limited to the practice of the one profession for which it was organized;
- no person or entity can be admitted as a member unless he, she, or it is qualified to practice the profession, and no interest can be sold except to someone so qualified; and,
- some states require members of professional LLCs to carry certain limits of malpractice insurance.

If you are forming a professional LLC, you should obtain a copy of the statute that governs them in your state. Also, check with the board that regulates your profession—they may have additional regulations that apply. Typically, the additional clauses would be worded like this:

No person may be admitted to membership who is not licensed to practice _____ in this state. No interest in this company may be sold to anyone who is not so licensed. Any member whose license to practice is revoked or terminated shall immediately terminate his or her membership.

Execution and Filing

Some states allow any person to sign an LLC's articles of organization (even an agent or attorney), but others require a member or all the members to sign. To avoid delay in case your state's rules have changed, you can have all members sign even if it does not appear that it is required.

Some states require the form to be signed in black ink, but it is advisable for everyone to do so in case your state recently adopted the requirement. Most also require typing or printing your name in addition to signing it.

Figure 4.3: **Additional Forms**

Some states require forms to be filed in addition to the articles of organization. The following states require the forms listed. These requirements may change, so check with your state for additional requirements.

Arizona	Affidavit of Publication
Arkansas	Franchise Tax Registration Form
California	Tax Voucher (form 3522)
District of Columbia	Consent of Registered Agent
Florida	*Certificate of Designation of Registered Agent
Georgia	Transmittal Form 231
Louisiana	Initial Report
Maine	*Acceptance of Appointment as Registered Agent
Michigan	If Form C&S 700 is not used for your articles, it must accompany your articles
New Hampshire	Addendum to Certificate of Formation
New York	Affidavit of Publication
North Dakota	Registered Agent Consent to Serve
Ohio	Original Appointment of Agent
Pennsylvania	Docketing Statement DSCB: 15-134A
South Dakota	First Annual Report
Wyoming	Consent to Appointment of Registered Agent

*The information on these forms can be incorporated into the articles, in which case the separate form does not need to be filed.

Some states return the form quickly, while others normally take several weeks but will file it quicker for an additional charge. Some provide a street address for courier service (FedEx, Airborne) and will return by courier if you prepay.

Publication

A few states require a new LLC to publish notice of formation in a newspaper. Usually, this must be in a *newspaper of general circulation*. In most cases, a small inexpensive newspaper, or *shopper*, can be used that will save hundreds of dollars over the rates of a big city daily newspaper. (Check the page for your state in Appendix A for the requirements.)

Membership or Management Agreement

An LLC must decide if it will be managed by all the members or by a limited number of managers. If it is to be run by managers, there may be one or more and he or she may be a member or not a member.

It is important, in either case, to have a written agreement spelling out the rights and duties of the members and managers, if any. This is also a good document in which to include other rules governing the LLC. Even if an LLC has only one member, a membership agreement should be signed to formalize the LLC and make it clear that the member is not personally liable for the debts of the business.

The law of LLCs is very new, and since corporations that do not follow procedures can have their veil pierced (and their shareholders held liable), it is possible that a court may try the same with an LLC. So following the old formula is the safest. Of course, if you set up procedures and do not follow them, this could backfire and a court could use that as a reason to impose liability.

Figure 4.4: **Membership Operating Agreement**

If your LLC will have one member or if it will have two or more members and be managed by all the members, you can use a generic member-managed operations agreement like this blank sample.

Limited Liability Company Member-Managed Operating Agreement of
_____, LLC

THIS AGREEMENT is made effective as of _____, 2007 between the members and the company.

1. Formation. A limited liability company of the above name has been formed under the laws of the state of _____ by filing articles of organization with the secretary of state. The purpose of the business shall be to carry on any act or activity lawful under the jurisdiction in which it operates. The company may operate under a fictitious name or names as long as the company is in compliance with applicable fictitious name registration laws. The term of the company shall be perpetual or until dissolved as provided by law or by vote of the members as provided in this agreement. Upon dissolution the remaining members shall have the power to continue the operation of the company as long as necessary and allowable under state law until the winding up of the affairs of the business has been completed.

2. Members. The initial members shall be listed on Schedule A, which shall accompany and be made a part of this agreement. Additional members may be admitted to membership upon the unanimous consent of the current members. Transfer or pledge of a member's interest may not be made except upon consent of all members.

3. Contributions. The initial capital contributions shall be listed on Schedule A, which shall accompany and be made a part of this agreement. No member shall be obligated to contribute any more than the amount set forth on Schedule A unless agreed to in writing by all of the members and no member shall have any personal liability for any debt, obligation or liability of the company other than for full payment of his or her capital contribution. No member shall be entitled to interest on the capital contribution. Member voting rights shall be in proportion to the amount of their contributions.

4. Business Purpose. The company has been organized for the business purpose of _____ .
_____

5. Profit and Loss. The profits and losses of the business, and all other taxable or deductible items shall be allocated to the members according to the percentages on Schedule A, which shall accompany and be made a part of this agreement.

6. Distributions. The company shall have the power to make distributions to its members in such amounts and at such intervals as a majority of the members deem appropriate according to law.

7. Management. The limited liability company shall be managed by its members listed on Schedule A. In the event of a dispute between members, final determination shall be made with a vote by the members, votes being proportioned according to capital contributions.

8. Fiduciary Duty. Each member of the company shall have a fiduciary duty to each other member and to the company to act in the best interests of the company in all dealing with and for the company.

9. Registered Agent. The company shall at all times have a registered agent and registered office. The initial registered agent and registered office shall be listed on Schedule A, which shall accompany and be made a part of this agreement.

10. Assets. The assets of the company shall be registered in the legal name of the company and not in the names of the individual members.

11. Records and Accounting. The company shall keep an accurate accounting of its affairs using any method of accounting allowed by law. All members shall have a right to inspect the records during normal business hours. The members shall have the power to hire such accountants as they deem necessary or desirable.

12. Banking. The members of the company shall be authorized to set up bank accounts as in their sole discretion are deemed necessary and are authorized to execute any banking resolutions provided by the institution in which the accounts are being set up.

13. Taxes. The company shall file such tax returns as required by law. The company shall elect to be taxed as a majority of the members decide is in their best interests. The "tax matters partner," as required by the Internal Revenue Code, shall be listed on Schedule A, which shall accompany and be made a part of this agreement.

14. Separate Entity. The company is a legal entity separate from its members. No member shall have any separate liability for any debts, obligations or liability of the company except as provided in this agreement.

15. Indemnity and Exculpation. The limited liability company shall indemnify and hold harmless its members, managers, employees and agents to the fullest extent allowed by law for acts or omissions done as part of their duties to or for the company. Indemnification shall include all liabilities, expenses, attorney and accountant fees, and other costs reasonably expended. No member shall be liable to the company for acts done in good faith.

16. Meetings. The company shall have no obligation to hold annual or any other meeting, but may hold such meetings if deemed necessary or desirable. However, each member shall participate in the management and decisions of the company. When meetings are held, each member of the company shall attend. No member shall be required to take any action which would result in personal liability for that member.

17. Executive Contract. The parties desire that this agreement shall constitute an executive contract under 1 U.S.C. §365.

18. Amendment of this Agreement. This agreement may not be amended except in writing signed by all of the members.

19. Conflict of Interest. No member shall be involved with any business or undertaking which competes with the interests of the company except upon agreement in writing by all of the members.

20. Deadlock. In the event that the members cannot come to an agreement on any matter the members agree to submit the issue to mediation to be paid for by the company. In the event the mediation is unsuccessful, they agree to seek arbitration under the rules of the American Arbitration Association.

21. Dissociation of a Member. A member shall have the right to discontinue membership upon giving thirty days notice. A member shall cease to have the right to membership upon death, court-ordered incapacity, bankruptcy or expulsion. The company shall have the right to buy the interest of any dissociated member at fair market value.

22. Dissolution. The company shall dissolve upon the unanimous consent of all the members or upon any event requiring dissolution under state law. In the event of the death, bankruptcy, permanent incapacity, or withdrawal of a member the remaining members may elect to dissolve or to continue the continuation of the company.

23. General Provisions. This agreement is intended to represent the entire agreement between the parties. In the event that any party of this agreement is held to be contrary to law or unenforceable, said party shall be considered amended to comply with the law and such holding shall not affect the enforceability of other terms of this agreement. This agreement shall be binding upon the heirs, successors and assigns of the members.

24. Miscellaneous. _____
_____
_____
_____
_____

IN WITNESS whereof, the members of the limited liability company sign this agreement and adopt it as their operating agreement.

Figure 4.5: **Management Operating Agreement**

If your LLC will have two or more members and be managed by a limited number of members or by someone who is not a member, you can use a generic management operating agreement like this blank sample.

Limited Liability Company Management Operating Agreement of
_____, LLC

THIS AGREEMENT is made effective as of _____, 2006 between the members and the company.

1. Formation. A limited liability company of the above name has been formed under the laws of the state of _____ by filing articles of organization with the secretary of state. The purpose of the business shall be to carry on any act or activity lawful under the jurisdiction in which it operates. The company may operate under a fictitious name or names as long as the company is in compliance with applicable fictitious name registration laws. The term of the company shall be perpetual or until dissolved as provided by law or by vote of the members as provided in this agreement. Upon dissolution the remaining members shall have the power to continue the operation of the company as long as necessary and allowable under state law until the winding up of the affairs of the business has been completed.

2. Members. The initial members shall be listed on Schedule A, which shall accompany and be made a part of this agreement. Additional members may be admitted to membership upon the unanimous consent of the current members. Transfer or pledge of a member's interest may not be made except upon consent of all members.

3. Contributions. The initial capital contributions shall be listed on Schedule A, which shall accompany and be made a part of this agreement. No member shall be obligated to contribute any more than the amount set forth on Schedule A unless agreed to in writing by all of the members and managers and no member shall have any personal liability for any debt, obligation or liability of the company other than for full payment of his or her capital contribution. No member shall be entitled to interest on the capital contribution. Member voting rights shall be in proportion to the amount of their contributions.

4. Business Purpose. The company has been organized for the business purpose of _____
_____.

5. Profit and Loss. The profits and losses of the business, and all other taxable or deductible items shall be allocated to the members according to the percentages on Schedule A, which shall accompany and be made a part of this agreement.

6. Distributions. The company shall have the power to make distributions to its members in such amounts and at such intervals as a majority of the members deem appropriate according to law.

7. Management. The limited liability company shall be managed by the managers listed on Schedule A, which shall accompany and be made a part of this agreement. These managers may or may not be members of the company and each manager shall have an equal vote with other managers as to management decisions. Managers shall serve until resignation or death or until they are removed by a majority vote of the members. Replacement managers shall be selected by a majority vote of the members. Managers shall have no personal liability for expenses, obligations or liabilities of the company.

8. Fiduciary Duty. Each member of the company shall have a fiduciary duty to each other member and to the company to act in the best interests of the company in all dealing with and for the company.

9. Registered Agent. The company shall at all times have a registered agent and registered office. The initial registered agent and registered office shall be listed on Schedule A, which shall accompany and be made a part of this agreement.

10. Assets. The assets of the company shall be registered in the legal name of the company and not in the names of the individual members.

11. Records and Accounting. The company shall keep an accurate accounting of its affairs using any method of accounting allowed by law. All members shall have a right to inspect the records during normal business hours. The members shall have the power to hire such accountants as they deem necessary or desirable.

12. Banking. The members of the company shall be authorized to set up bank accounts as in their sole discretion are deemed necessary and are authorized to execute any banking resolutions provided by the institution in which the accounts are being set up.

13. Taxes. The company shall file such tax returns as required by law. The company shall elect to be taxed as a majority of the members decide is in their best interests. The "tax matters partner," as required by the Internal Revenue Code, shall be listed on Schedule A, which shall accompany and be made a part of this agreement.

14. Separate Entity. The company is a legal entity separate from its members. No member shall have any separate liability for any debts, obligations or liability of the company except as provided in this agreement.

15. Indemnity and Exculpation. The limited liability company shall indemnify and hold harmless its members, managers, employees and agents to the fullest extent allowed by law for acts or omissions done as part of their duties to or for the company. Indemnification shall include all liabilities, expenses, attorney and accountant fees, and other costs reasonably expended. No member shall be liable to the company for acts done in good faith.

16. Meetings. The company shall have no obligation to hold annual or any other meeting, but may hold such meetings if deemed necessary or desirable. However, each member shall participate in the management and decisions of the company. When meetings are held, each member of the company shall attend. No member shall be required to take any action which would result in personal liability for that member.

17. Executive Contract. The parties desire that this agreement shall constitute an executive contract under 1 U.S.C. §365.

18. Amendment of this Agreement. This agreement may not be amended except in writing signed by all of the members.

19. Conflict of Interest. No member shall be involved with any business or undertaking which competes with the interests of the company except upon agreement in writing by all of the members.

20. Deadlock. In the event that the members cannot come to an agreement on any matter the members agree to submit the issue to mediation to be paid for by the company. In the event the mediation is unsuccessful, they agree to seek arbitration under the rules of the American Arbitration Association.

21. Dissociation of a Member. A member shall have the right to discontinue membership upon giving thirty days notice. A member shall cease to have the right to membership upon death, court-ordered incapacity, bankruptcy or expulsion. The company shall have the right to buy the interest of any dissociated member at fair market value.

22. Dissolution. The company shall dissolve upon the unanimous consent of all the members or upon any event requiring dissolution under state law. In the event of the death, bankruptcy, permanent incapacity, or withdrawal of a member the remaining members may elect to dissolve or to continue the continuation of the company.

23. General Provisions. This agreement is intended to represent the entire agreement between the parties. In the event that any party of this agreement is held to be contrary to law or unenforceable, said party shall be considered amended to comply with the law and such holding shall not affect the enforceability of other terms of this agreement. This agreement shall be binding upon the heirs, successors and assigns of the members.

24. Miscellaneous. _____
_____
_____
_____
_____

IN WITNESS whereof, the members of the limited liability company sign this agreement and adopt it as their operating agreement.

_____   _____

_____   _____

The undersigned accepts the position of manager and all of the responsibilities and duties thereof.

_____
_____, Manager

Capitalization

Your new company will naturally need some money to get operations started. Some of this will be *capital* that you put into the business, but some may also be loans. Money that is set up as a loan can be later taken out tax-free. Therefore, it might seem good to start with all loans and little or no capital. The danger is, if a business is *undercapitalized*, the owners may later be liable for some of its debts.

"What is enough capital for a business?" is a legal question, and no one can say what a judge or jury may some day decide. If the business is a service company and needs little equipment other than ladders or computers, a couple thousand dollars would be fine. If the business needs a lot of expensive equipment, it would probably not be reasonable to put in $1,000 in capital and $99,000 in loans.

One way to know what is reasonable is to see what a bank would loan the company. If a company could put $5,000 down on its start-up equipment and borrow the rest, it would probably be reasonable to use $5,000 as capital and $95,000 as a loan from the owner.

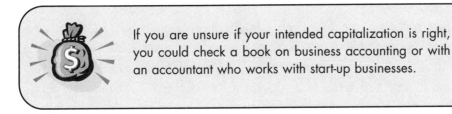

If you are unsure if your intended capitalization is right, you could check a book on business accounting or with an accountant who works with start-up businesses.

If an existing business is being converted to an LLC, you may want to contribute the existing equipment as part, or all, of the start-up capital. To avoid potential liability, you should be sure not to value the equipment at more than the fair market value.

In some instances, people wish to trade services for an interest in a business. For example, one person may contribute business equipment and the other work for three months without pay, for fifty-fifty ownership in the business. In some states, this is not allowed. Check your state statute before setting up such an arrangement.

Tax Forms

In forming an LLC, there are two tax forms you will need to complete—IRS Form SS-4 and IRS Form 8832. All Internal Revenue Service (IRS) forms can be obtained at **www.irs.gov**.

Taxpayer Identification Number

Prior to opening a bank account, the limited liability company must obtain a *taxpayer identification number*—the business equivalent of a Social Security number. The fastest way to get the number is to obtain it online. (If the IRS website is not running properly, you may need to follow up with a phone call to get the number.) Get the form at **www.irs.gov** by entering "SS-4" in the search box.

You can also get the number by filing IRS Form SS-4. If you mail it in, it may take two or three weeks. If you fax it in, they will usually fax your number in a few days. If you need the number more quickly, you can obtain it by phone in twenty to forty minutes, depending on how long you are on hold. Be sure to have your completed IRS Form SS-4 in front of you when you call. The address, phone, and fax numbers are in the instructions with the form.

When you apply for this number, you will probably be put on the mailing list for other tax forms. If you do not receive these, you should call your local IRS forms number and request the forms for new businesses. These include Circular E (explaining the taxes due), the W-4 forms for each employee, the tax deposit coupons, and the Form 941 quarterly return for withholding.

Form 8832

IRS Form 8832 was issued by the IRS in 1997 to allow LLCs to chose their tax status. It is essentially a choice between partnership taxation and corporate taxation. For a single-member LLC, it is a choice between sole proprietorship taxation and corporate taxation.

The difference in taxation is that a sole proprietorship or partnership is not taxed at all, but a corporation is treated like a separate taxpayer. A sole proprietorship or partnership reports its income and expenses and the proprietor or partners report the net profit or loss on their personal tax return. A corporation files a tax return and pays tax on any profits, and if it distributes any of the profits to the members, those profits are taxed again. Therefore, in most cases it is better to choose partnership taxation.

One way around the double taxation is if all of the profits can be paid to the members as salary, they are deductible and the corporation has no profit on which to pay tax. The problem arises when the company makes more money than would be reasonable to pay as salaries. The IRS can then impose extra corporate taxation on the excess amounts.

If you are unsure how you wish to be taxed, you should consult a book on taxation of businesses or check with a tax professional. Once you decide, you should complete IRS Form 8832. If you elect to pass through taxation, you do not need to file the form—just give it to the members to file with their annual returns. If you elect corporate taxation, you need to file the form within seventy-five days of organization.

Form 2553

If you elect to be taxed as a corporation, and if you would like that to be S corporation status rather than C corporation status, then you must file Form 2553 within seventy-five days of starting your business.

Employees

An LLC that has employees other than its members is subject to numerous laws and reporting requirements that are beyond the scope of this book. These include new hire reporting, federal wage withholding, state and federal unemployment compensation taxes, discrimination laws, minimum wage laws, and numerous posters that must be placed in the workplace regarding child labor laws and health and safety issues. Check federal and state laws. A 2007 federal tax case ruled that when an LLC is taxed like a partnership or proprietorship its members can be held personally liable for employment taxes.

Bank Accounts

A limited liability company must have a bank account. Checks payable to a limited liability company cannot be cashed—they must be deposited into an account.

Unfortunately, many banks charge companies for the right to put their money in the bank. For similar balance and activity between a personal account and a corporate account, an individual might earn $6 interest for the month while a corporation pays $40 in bank fees. The bank is not losing money on every personal account, so the corporate account is simply generating $46 more in profit for the bank.

Fortunately, some banks have set up reasonable fees for small businesses, such as charging no fees if a balance of $1,000 or $2,500 is maintained. Because the fees can easily amount to hundreds of dollars a year, it pays to shop around. Even if the bank is relatively far from the business, using bank-by-mail can make the distance meaningless. However, do not be surprised if a bank raises its initial low fees. A company could change banks four times in one year as each one raises its fees or is bought out by a bank with higher fees.

One method for avoiding high bank fees is to open a checking account and a *money market account.* (Money market accounts pay higher interest and usually do not charge for making deposits. You can only write three checks a month, but you can usually make unlimited withdrawals.) Make all of your deposits into the money market account and pay bills out of the regular checking account, transferring funds as needed. Some banks also charge for deposits into money market accounts, so start one at a brokerage firm.

Another way to save money is to order checks from a private source rather than through the bank. These are usually much cheaper than those the bank offers because the bank makes a profit on the check printing. If the bank officer does not like the idea when you are opening the account, just wait until your first batch runs out and switch over without telling the bank. They probably will not notice, as long as you get the checks printed correctly. Most *business checks* are large and expensive. There is no reason you cannot use small *personal size checks* for your business.

Licenses

Counties and municipalities in most states are authorized to levy a license tax on the right to do business. Before opening your business, you should obtain a county occupational license, and if you will be working within a city, a city occupational license. Businesses that work in several cities, such as builders, must obtain a license from each city in which they will work. This does not have to be done until you actually begin a job in a particular city.

County occupational licenses can usually be obtained from the tax collector in the county courthouse. City licenses are usually available at city hall. Be sure to find out if zoning allows your type of business before buying or leasing property, because the licensing departments will check the zoning before issuing your license.

Problems occasionally arise when a person attempts to start a business in his or her home. New small businesses cannot afford to pay rent for commercial space and cities often try to forbid business in residential areas. Getting a county occupational license often gives notice to the city that a business is being conducted in a residential area.

Some people avoid the problem by starting their businesses without occupational licenses, figuring that the penalties are nowhere near the cost of office space. Others get the county license and ignore the city rules. If a person has commercial trucks and equipment parked on his or her property, there will probably be complaints by neighbors, and the city will most likely take legal action. However, if a person's business consists merely of making phone calls out of the home and keeping supplies inside the house, the problem may never arise.

If a problem does occur regarding a home business that does not disturb the neighbors, a good argument can be made that the zoning law is unconstitutional. When zoning laws were first instituted, they were not meant to stop people from doing things in a residence that had historically been part of the life in a residence. Consider a painter. Should a zoning law prohibit a person from sitting in his or her home and painting pictures? If he or she sells them for a living, is there a difference? Can the government force him or her to rent commercial space?

Similar arguments can be made for many home businesses, but court battles with a city are expensive and probably not worth the effort for a small business. The best course of action is to keep a low profile. Using a post office box is sometimes helpful in diverting attention away from the residence. However, the Secretary of State and the occupational license administrator will usually demand a street address. In most areas, there should be no problem using a residential address. As always, check with your state's individual laws before committing to anything.

Figure 4.6: **Checklist for Forming an LLC**

☐ Decide on a company name

☐ Search the name to be sure it is not already taken

☐ Prepare and file Articles of Organization and any other organizational form required by the state

☐ Decide on capitalization and tax status

☐ Obtain federal Employer Identification Number (IRS Form SS-4)

☐ Prepare IRS Form 8832 and file it within seventy-five days if you are choosing corporate taxation

☐ Prepare and file Form 2553 if S corporation status is desired (file within seventy-five days of start-up)

☐ Prepare Membership Operating Agreement or Management Operating Agreement

☐ If necessary, meet with securities lawyer regarding nonparticipating members

☐ Hold organizational meeting

  ☐ Complete Operating Agreement

  ☐ Complete Bill of Sale if property is traded for interest

☐ File fictitious or assumed name registration if one will be used

☐ Get city or county licenses, if needed

☐ Open bank account

Chapter 5

Membership Interests in an LLC

Before setting up your limited liability company (LLC), you need to determine its financial structure as well as a plan for future expansion.

Capital Structure

There is no hard and fast rule as to how much capital you should put into a limited liability company. The more you assign as capital, the more you have at risk in the business. Therefore, you want to deposit as little as possible. Keep in mind that if you contribute too little, a court might some day say you were undercapitalized and find you personally liable for company debts, just as it could for a corporation. Also, there could be tax problems with not counting enough of your contributions as capital or for contributing appreciated property. These matters should be discussed with a tax specialist.

If you are starting a small business that does not need a lot of expensive equipment, a few thousand dollars would be a safe amount with which to start. If you need to buy expensive equipment, and the company can borrow the money from a third party to cover it, you would probably be safe as well. However, if you need to purchase expensive equipment and personally loan the money to the company rather than contribute it as capital, you should weigh the risks of a lawsuit and consider consulting an attorney or accountant who specializes in business start-ups.

One thing to keep in mind is that if you do not put in the amount of capital stated in your initial agreement and are later sued or file bankruptcy, you may be required to come up with any unpaid amount because it may be considered an unpaid debt to the company. That is something for which you could be held personally liable. In a grievous case, a judge might use it as a reason to void the limited liability of the LLC.

Payment for Membership Interests

Most states allow membership interests to be paid with money, property, services, or a promissory note. The important thing to remember is if a member fails to make the specified payment or takes the money back out (other than salary or profit), he or she may be liable to the company or its creditors for the full amount that should have been paid.

Some other things to consider include the following.

- If a member trades services for an interest in the capital of the company, he or she must pay income tax on the value of interest at the time the services are exchanged for the interest. (If the interest is only a share of future profits, the tax does not have to be paid until the profits are received.)
- When appreciated property is traded to an LLC in exchange for a membership interest, the tax basis of the property carries over to the

membership interest. Taxes on the appreciation are paid when the member sells his or her LLC interest.

- If the LLC sells the property, it may have to pay a tax on the amount received over the contributor's basis.

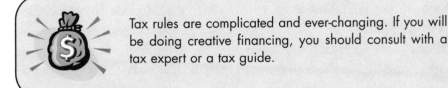

Tax rules are complicated and ever-changing. If you will be doing creative financing, you should consult with a tax expert or a tax guide.

Securities Laws

The issuance of *securities* is subject to both federal and state securities laws. A *security* can either be an equity interest in a company (stock, membership) or debt (notes, bonds, etc.). The laws covering securities are so broad that any instrument representing an investment in an enterprise where the investor is relying on the efforts of others for profit is considered a security. Even a *promissory note* has been held to be a security. Once an investment is determined to involve a security, strict rules apply. If the rules are not followed, there can be criminal penalties and civil damages can be awarded to purchasers.

The rules are designed to protect people who put up money as an investment in a business. In the stock market crash of 1929, many people lost their life savings in swindles, and the government wants to be sure that it will not happen again. Unfortunately, these laws can also make it difficult to raise capital for many honest businesses.

The goal of the laws covering sales of securities is that investors be given full disclosure of the risks involved in an investment. To accomplish this, the law usually requires that the securities must either be registered with the federal *Securities and Exchange Commission* (SEC) or a similar state regulatory body, and that lengthy disclosure statements be compiled and distributed.

The law is complicated and strict compliance is required. The penalties are so harsh that most lawyers will not handle securities matters. You most likely would not be able to get through the registration process on your own. Still, like your decision to form your LLC without a lawyer, you may wish to consider some alternatives when attempting to raise capital without a lawyer.

- Borrow the money as a personal loan from friends or relatives. The disadvantage is that you will have to pay them back personally if the business fails. However, you may have to do that anyway if they are close relatives or if you do not follow the securities laws.
- Tailor your stock issuance to fall within the exemptions in the securities laws. There are some exemptions in the securities laws for small businesses that may apply to your transaction. (The anti-fraud provisions always apply even if the transaction is exempt from registration.) Some exemptions are explained on the following pages, but you should make at least one appointment with a securities lawyer to be sure you have covered everything and that there have not been any changes in the law. Often, you can pay for an hour or so of a securities lawyer's time for $100 or $200 and ask questions about your plans. He or she can tell you what not to do and what your options are. You can then make an informed decision.

Federal Exemptions from Securities Laws

In most situations where one person, a husband and wife, or a few partners run a business, and all parties are active in the enterprise, securities laws do not apply to their issuance of membership interests to themselves. As a practical matter, if a relative of yours wants to put up some money for some stock in your business, you might not get in trouble. They probably will not seek triple damages and criminal penalties if your business fails.

However, you may wish to obtain money from additional investors to enable your business to grow. This can be done in many circumstances as long as you follow the rules carefully. In some cases, you do not have to file anything with the Securities and Exchange Commission (SEC), but in others, you must file a notice.

Federal Private Placement Exemption

If you sell interests in your business to a small group of people without any advertising, you can fall into the private offering exemption if the following are true:

- all persons to whom offers are made are financially astute, are participants in the business, or have a substantial net worth;
- no advertising or general solicitation is used to promote the stock;
- the number of persons to whom the offers are made is limited;
- the shares are purchased for investment and not for immediate resale;
- the persons to whom the interest is offered are given all relevant information (including financial information) regarding the issuance and the corporation. Again, there are numerous court cases explaining each aspect of these rules, including such questions as what defines a *financially astute* person; and,
- a filing claiming the exemption is made upon the United States Securities and Exchange Commission.

Federal Intrastate Offering Exemption

If you only offer your securities to residents of one state, you may be exempt from federal securities laws. This is because federal laws usually only apply to interstate commerce. Intrastate offerings are covered by SEC Rule 147, and if it is followed carefully, your sale will be exempt from federal registration.

Federal Small Offerings Exemptions

In recent years, the SEC has liberalized the rules in order to make it easier for business to grow. Under Regulation D adopted by the Securities and Exchange Commission, there are three types of exemptions under rules 504, 505, and 506.

- Under SEC Rule 504, the offering of securities of up to $1,000,000 in a twelve-month period can be exempt. Offers can be made to any number of persons, no specific information must be provided, and investors do not have to be sophisticated.

- Under SEC Rule 505, offerings of up to $5,000,000 can be made in a twelve-month period, but no public advertising may be used, and only thirty-five non-accredited investors may purchase stock. Any number of accredited investors may purchase stock. (Accredited investors are sophisticated individuals with high net worth or high income, large trusts or investment companies, or persons involved in the business.)
- Under SEC Rule 506, there is no limit on the amount of money that may be raised, but like Rule 505, it does not allow advertising and limits non-accredited investors to thirty-five.

State Securities Laws

One reason there are exemptions from federal securities laws is there are so many state laws covering securities that additional registration is not needed. Every state has securities laws, called *blue sky laws*. If you wish to offer your stock in all fifty states, you must be registered in all fifty states unless you can fit into one of the exemptions. However, exemptions are very limited.

Typical State Law Private Placement Exemption

The most common exemption is the private placement exemption. This can apply if all of the following are true:

- there are thirty-five or fewer purchasers of shares;
- no commissions are paid to anyone to promote the stock;
- no advertising or general solicitation is used to promote the stock;
- all material information (including financial information) regarding the stock issuance and the company is given or is accessible to all shareholders; and,
- a three-day right of recision is given.

These rules may sound simple, but there are many more rules, regulations, and court cases explaining each one in more detail. For example, what does "thirty-five persons" mean? It sounds simple, but it can mean more than thirty-five persons. Spouses, persons whose net worth exceeds a million dollars, and founders of the company may not be counted in some circumstances.

As you can see, the exemption does not give you much latitude in raising money. Therefore, if you wish to raise money from a wider group of people, you will have to register. To find out more about your state's requirements, contact the securities commission of your state. The address can be found in Figure 5.1.

Blue Sky Reporter

Another good source of information concerning the securities laws of all fifty states is the *Blue Sky Reporter*, a multi-volume loose leaf service that summarizes the securities laws of the states. A copy should be available in most law libraries.

QUICK Tip

You can link to the securities laws of each state through the website of the North American Securities Administrators Association, Inc., located at **www.nasaa.org**.

Internet Stock Sales

With the advent of the Internet, promoters of business interests have a new way of reaching large numbers of people. However, all securities laws apply to the Internet, and they are being enforced. Recently, state attorney generals have issued cease and desist orders to promoters not registered in their states.

Under current law, you must be registered in a state in order to sell stock to its residents. You must turn down any residents who want to buy your stock if you are not registered in that state.

QUICK Tip

Some Internet sites that may be helpful in raising capital are:

America's Business Funding Directory: www.businessfinance.com
Angel Capital Electronic Network (SBA): www.sba.gov
FinanceHub: www.financehub.com
NVST: www.nvst.com

Payment for Membership Interests

When issuing stock, it is important that full payment be made by the purchasers. If the shares have a par value, and the payment is cash, the cash must not be less than the par value. In most states, promissory notes cannot be used in payment for shares. The shares must not be issued until the payment has been received by the corporation.

Trading Property for Interests

In many cases, organizers of a corporation have property they want to contribute for use in starting up the business. This is often the case when an ongoing business is incorporated. To avoid future problems, the property should be traded at a fair value for the shares, and the directors should pass a resolution stating that they agree with the value of the property. When the stock certificate is issued in exchange for the property, a bill of sale should be executed by the owner of the property detailing everything that is being exchanged for the stock.

Taxable Transactions

In cases where property is exchanged for something of value, such as stock, there is often income tax due as if there had been a sale of the property. Fortunately, Section 351 of the IRS Code allows tax-free exchange of property for stock, if the persons receiving the stock for the property or for cash *end up owning* at least 80% of the voting and other stock in the corporation. If more than 20% of the stock is issued in exchange for services instead of property or cash, the transfers of property will be taxable and treated as sales for cash.

Trading Services for Interests

In some cases, the founders of an LLC wish to issue membership interests to one or more persons in exchange for their services to the business. It has always been possible to issue interests for services that have previously been performed. Some states make it unlawful to issue interests for promises to perform services in the future. Check your state's LLC statute if you plan to do this.

Figure 5.1: **State Securities Registration Offices**

The following are the addresses of the state offices that handle registration of securities. You can contact them for information on their requirements.

Alabama Securities Commission
770 Washington Street
Suite 570
Montgomery, AL 36130
Phone: 334-242-2984 or 800-222-1253
Fax: 334-242-0240 or 334-353-4690
www.asc.state.al.us

**Alaska Department of Commerce
and Economic Development
Division of Banking, Securities,
and Corporations**
P.O. Box 110807
Juneau, AK 99811
Phone: 907-465-2521
Fax: 907-465-2549
www.dced.state.ak.us/bsc

**Arizona Corporation Commission
Securities Division**
1300 West Washington Street
3rd Floor
Phoenix, AZ 85007
Phone: 602-542-4242
Fax: 602-594-7470
www.ccsd.cc.state.az.us

Arkansas Securities Department
Heritage West Building
201 East Markham
3rd Floor
Little Rock, AR 72201
Phone: 501-324-9260
Fax: 501-324-9268

**California Department of
Corporations
Securities Regulation Division**
320 West 4th Street
Suite 750
Los Angeles, CA 90013
Phone: 213-576-7500
Fax: 213-576-7179
www.corp.ca.gov/srd/security.htm

Colorado Division of Securities
1580 Lincoln Street
Suite 420
Denver, CO 80203
Phone: 303-894-2320
Fax: 303-861-2126
www.dora.state.co.us/securities

Connecticut Securities Division
260 Constitution Plaza
Hartford, CT 06103
Phone: 860-240-8230
Fax: 860-240-8295
www.state.ct.us/dob

**Delaware Department of Justice
Division of Securities**
820 North French Street, 5th Floor
Wilmington, DE 19801
Phone: 302-577-8242
Fax: 302-577-6987
www.state.de.us/securities/index.htm

**District of Columbia
Department of Insurance and
Securities Regulation**
810 First Street
Suite 701
Washington, DC 20002
Phone: 202-727-8000
Fax: 202-535-1196
http://disb.dc.gov/disr/site/default.asp

**Florida Division of Securities and
Finance**
200 East Gaines Street
Tallahassee, FL 32399
Phone: 850-410-9805
Fax: 850-410-9748
www.dbf.state.fl.us/licensing

**Georgia Secretary of State
Securities and Business
Regulation Division**
2 Martin Luther King Jr. Drive, S.E.
Suite 802, West Tower
Atlanta, GA 30334
Phone: 404-656-3920
Fax: 404-657-8410
www.sos.state.ga.us/securities
or www.georgiasecurities.org

**Hawaii Department of Commerce
and Consumer Affairs
Commissioner of Securities**
P. O. Box 40
Honolulu, HI 96810
Phone: 808-586-2744
Fax: 808-586-3977
www.hawaii.gov/dcca/areas/sec

Idaho Department of Finance
700 West State Street
2nd Floor
P.O. Box 83702
Boise, ID 83720
Phone: 208-332-8000
Fax: 208-332-8099
http://finance.state.id.us

Illinois Securities Department
Jefferson Terrace
Suite 300 A
300 West Jefferson Street
Springfield, IL 62702
Phone: 217-782-2256
Fax: 217-782-8876
www.sos.state.il.us/departments/
   securities/home.html

Indiana Securities Division
302 West Washington Street
Room E-111
Indianapolis, IN 46204
Phone: 317-232-6681 or 800-223-8791
Fax: 317-233-3675
www.IN.gov/sos/securities

Iowa Securities Bureau
340 Maple Street
Des Moines, IA 50319
Phone: 515-281-4441
Fax: 515-281-3059
www.iowa.gov

**Kansas Securities Commissioner
Office of the Securities
Commissioner**
618 South Kansas Avenue
Topeka, KS 66603
Phone: 785-296-3307
Fax: 785-296-6872
www.securities.state.ks.us

**Kentucky Department of Financial
Institutions**
1025 Capital Center Drive
Suite 200
Frankfort, KY 40601
Phone: 502-573-3390 or 800-223-2579
Fax: 502-573-8787
www.dfi.state.ky.us

**Louisiana Office of Financial
Institutions
Securities Division
Commissioner of Securities**
8660 United Plaza Boulevard
2nd Floor
Baton Rouge, LA 70809
Phone: 225-925-4660
Fax: 225-925-4548
www.ofi.state.la.us

**Maine Department of
Professional and
Financial Regulation
Office of Securities**
121 State House Station
Augusta, ME 04333
Phone: 207-624-8551
Fax: 207-624-8590
www.state.me.us/pfr/sec/sec_index.htm

Maryland Securities Division
200 Saint Paul Place
Baltimore, MD 21202
Phone: 410-576-6360
www.oag.state.md.us/securities/
    index.htm

Massachusetts Securities Division
One Ashburton Place
17th Floor
Boston, MA 02108
Phone: 617-727-3548 or 800-269-5428
Fax: 617-248-0177
www.state.ma.us/sec/sct/sctidx.htm

**Michigan Department of
Consumer and Industry Services
Offices of Financial and Insurance
Services**
P.O. Box 30220
Lansing, MI 48909
Phone: 517-373-0220 or 877-999-6442
Fax: 517-335-4978
www.michigan.gov/cis

**Minnesota Department of
Commerce**
85 7th Place East
Suite 500
St. Paul, MN 55101
Phone: 651-296-4973
www.state.mn.us

Mississippi Securities Division
P.O. Box 136
Jackson, MS 39205
Phone: 800-804-6364
Fax: 601-359-2663
www.sos.state.ms.us

**Office of the Missouri
Secretary of State
Securities Division**
600 West Main Street
2nd Floor
Jefferson City, MO 65101
Phone: 573-751-4136
Fax: 573-526-3124
www.sos.mo.gov/securities

**Montana Office of the
State Auditor
Securities Division**
840 Helena Avenue
Helena, MT 59601
Phone: 406-444-3246
Fax: 406-444-3497
www.discoveringmontana.com/sao/
  securities

**Nebraska Bureau of Securities
Commerce Court**
1230 "O" Street
Suite 400
P.O. Box 95006
Lincoln, NE 68509
Phone: 402-471-3445
www.ndbf.org

Nevada Securities Division
555 East Washington Avenue
Suite 5200
Las Vegas, NV 89101
Phone: 702-486-2440
Fax: 702-486-2452
www.sos.state.nv.us/securities/index.htm

**New Hampshire Bureau of
Securities Regulation**
State House
Room 204
Concord, NH 03301
Phone: 603-271-1463
Fax: 603-271-7933
webster.state.nh.us/sos/securities

New Jersey Bureau of Securities
P.O. Box 47029
Newark, NJ 07101
Phone: 973-504-3600
Fax: 973-504-3601
www.state.nj.us/lps/ca/bos.htm

**New Mexico Securities Division
Regulation and Licensing
Department**
2550 Cerrillos Road
3rd Floor
Santa Fe, NM 87505
Phone: 505-827-7010
Fax: 505-827-7095
www.rld.state.nm.us/sec/index.htm

**New York State
Attorney General's Office**
Investors and Securities
The Capitol
Albany, NY 12224
Phone: 212-416-8000
Fax: 212-416-8816
www.oag.state.ny.us/investors/
  investors.html

**North Carolina Securities Division
Department of the Secretary of
State**
P.O. Box 29622
Raleigh, NC 27626
Phone: 919-733-3924
Fax: 919-733-5172
www.secretary.state.nc.us/sec

**North Dakota Securities
Commission**
State Capitol
5th Floor
600 East Boulevard Avenue
Bismarck, ND 58505
Phone: 701-328-2910
Fax: 701-328-2946
www.ndsecurities.com

Ohio Department of Commerce Division of Securities
77 South High Street
22nd Floor
Columbus, OH 43215
Phone: 614-644-7381
www.securities.state.oh.us

Oklahoma Department of Securities
Suite 860, First National Center
120 North Robinson
Oklahoma City, OK 73102
Phone: 405-280-7700
Fax: 405-280-7742
www.securities.state.ok.us

Oregon Department of Consumer and Business Services Division of Finance and Corporate Securities
P.O. Box 14480
Salem, OR 97309
Phone: 503-378-4140
Fax: 503-947-7862
www.cbs.state.or.us/external/dfcs

Pennsylvania Division of Corporation Finance Pennsylvania Securities Commission
Eastgate Office Building
2nd Floor
1010 North 7th Street
Harrisburg, PA 17102
Phone: 717-787-8061
Fax: 717-783-5122
www.psc.state.pa.us

Puerto Rico Commissioner of Financial Institutions
Centro Europa Building
1492 Ponce de Leon Avenue
Suite 600
San Juan, PR 00907
Phone: 787-723-3131
Fax: 787-723-4255
www.cif.gov.pr/valores_eng.html

South Carolina Securities Division
P.O. Box 11549
Columbia, SC 29211
Phone: 803-734-9916
Fax: 803-734-3677
www.scsecurities.org/index.html

South Dakota Division of Securities
445 East Capitol Avenue
Pierre, SD 57501
Phone: 605-773-4823
Fax: 605-773-5953
www.state.sd.us/dcr/securities/
    security.htm

Tennessee Department of Commerce and Insurance Securities Division
500 James Robertson Parkway
Suite 680
Davy Crockett Tower
Nashville, TN 37243
Phone: 615-741-3187
Fax: 615-532-8375
www.state.tn.us/commerce

Texas State Securities Board
P.O. Box 13167
Austin, TX 78711
Phone: 512-305-8300
Fax: 512-305-8310
www.ssb.state.tx.us

Utah Department of Commerce Division of Securities
Box 146760
Salt Lake City, UT 84114
Phone: 801-530-6600
Fax: 801-530-6980
www.securities.state.ut.us

Vermont Securities Division Department of Banking, Insurance, Securities and Health Care Administration
89 Main Street
Drawer 20
Montpelier, VT 05620
Phone: 802-828-3420
www.bishca.state.vt.us/securitiesdiv/
    securindex.htm

Virginia State Corporation Commission
P.O. Box 1197
Richmond, VA 23218
Phone: 804-371-9967
Fax: 804-371-9911
www.scc.virginia.gov

Washington Department of Financial Institutions Securities Division
P.O. Box 9033
Olympia, WA 98507
Phone: 360-902-8760
Fax: 360-902-0524
www.dfi.wa.gov

West Virginia Securities Division
State Capitol Building 1
Room W-100
Charleston, WV 25305
Phone: 304-558-2257
Fax: 304-558-4211
www.wvauditor.com

Wisconsin Division of Securities
P.O. Box 8041
Madison, WI 53708
Phone: 608-264-7969
Fax: 608-264-7968
www.wdfi.org/fi/securities

Wyoming Securities Division Secretary of the State
The Capital Building
Room 109
200 West 24th Street
Cheyenne, WY 82002
Phone: 307-777-7370
Fax: 307-777-5339
http://soswy.state.wy.us/securiti/
    securiti.htm

Chapter

Running a Limited Liability Company

One benefit of the limited liability company is the lack of requirements needed to comply with the formalities of a corporation. It is not yet totally clear what, if any, requirements courts may impose. Though it is widely recognized that the requirements will be less strict than for a corporation, to be safe, it is best to have some formalities such as keeping minutes and records.

Day-to-Day Activities

As previously mentioned, every LLC should have an operating agreement. This usually contains some formalities for the operation of the company. The important thing is that, if there are formalities in the document, you should follow them.

Minutes

In most states, the keeping of *minutes* is not specifically required of an LLC, but it is a simple act that may be helpful in proving that the LLC followed enough formalities to be legitimate. Whenever the company takes some major action, such as leasing a new office or granting bonuses, you should prepare minutes reflecting the decision.

One important point to remember is to keep the company separate from your personal affairs. Do not continuously make loans to yourself from company funds, and do not commingle funds.

Another important point to remember is to always use the name of the company with the correct suffix (LLC, LC, etc.). Always sign company documents as a member of the company acting for the company, like this:

Happy Daze, LLC
By ___*Joe Daze*_____, Member

If you do not, you may lose your protection from liability. There have been cases where a person forgot to put his title after his name and was held personally liable for a company debt.

Member Meetings

There is no requirement for regular meetings of the members. However, once again, since the law is not settled in this area, the more formality you use, the greater protection you have.

Holding a meeting when major decisions are being made is a good idea. If you are a one-member company, you can hold the meeting in your head. Just remember to fill out a minutes form and put it with the company records.

Figure 6.1: Records

Each state has its own statute controlling whether records need to be kept, and if so, what types. Typically, the following types of things need to be kept on file:

▶ a current list of the names and last known addresses of all members;

▶ a copy of the articles of organization, plus any amendments;

▶ copies of the company's income tax returns for the last three years;

▶ copies of any regulations or member agreements currently in effect;

▶ copies of any financial statements for the company for the last three years; and,

▶ the amount of cash and the agreed value of any property or services contributed by each member or agreed to be contributed by each member.

Annual Reports

In most states, an LLC must file a report each year (or in some states, every two years). This is to let the state keep an up-to-date record of the status of the company, and in many states the fee is small. However, in some states, the annual report is a way to raise revenue, and the fee is hundreds of dollars.

In most states, the report is a preprinted form with the company name, address, and member names, which needs to be signed and returned.

Failure to file your annual report on time can result in your company being dissolved. In some states the fee for reinstatement is over $500, so do not miss the deadline.

Section II:

Corporations

Chapter 7

What a Corporation Is

A *corporation* is a legal *person* that can be created under state law. As a person, a corporation has certain rights and obligations, including the right to do business in its own name and the obligation to pay taxes. Some laws use the words "natural persons." A *natural person* refers only to human beings. A corporation can only be referred to as a "person" under the law, and is never referred to as a "natural person."

Business corporations were invented hundreds of years ago to promote risky ventures, such as voyages to explore the new world. Prior to the use of corporations, if a venture failed, persons who invested in it faced the possibility of unlimited liability. By using a corporation, many people were able to invest fixed sums of money for a new venture, and if the venture made money, they shared the profits. If the venture failed, the most they could lose was their initial investment.

The reasons for having a corporation are the same today. Corporations allow investors to put up money for new ventures without the risk of further liability. While our legal system is making people liable in more and more situations, the corporation remains one of the few shields from liability that has not yet been abandoned.

Before forming a corporation, you should be familiar with some common corporate terms that are used in the text.

Articles of Incorporation

The *articles of incorporation* (in some states referred to as the *charter* or the *certificate of incorporation*) is the document that is filed with the appropriate state agency to start the corporation. In all but twelve states, this agency is the secretary of state. In other states, it may be called the department of state, the division of corporations, or some similar name. For simplicity, the phrase "secretary of state" will be used to designate this agency in this book.

In most cases, the articles of incorporation legally needs to contain only five basic statements. Some corporations have lengthy articles of incorporation, but this just makes it harder to make changes in the corporate structure. It is usually better to keep the articles short and put the details in the bylaws.

Shareholder

A *shareholder* is a person who owns stock in a corporation. In most small corporations, the shareholders act as the officers and directors, but most shareholders do not have these roles in large corporations. Sometimes small corporations have shareholders who are not officers, such as when the stock is in one spouse's name and the other spouse runs the business. Specific laws regarding issuance of shares and shareholders' rights vary from state to state, and are listed in the various state statutes. Shareholders must meet once a year to elect directors and make other major decisions for the corporation.

Board of Directors

The *board of directors* is the controlling body of a corporation that makes major corporate decisions and elects the officers. It usually meets just once a year. In most states, a corporation can have one director (who can also hold all offices and own all the stock). In a small corporation, the board members are usually also officers.

Officers

The *officers* of a corporation usually include a president, secretary, treasurer, and vice president. These persons typically run the day-to-day affairs of the business. They are elected each year by the board of directors. In most states, one person can hold all of the offices of a corporation.

Registered Agent

The *registered agent* (in some states referred to as the *resident agent*) is the person designated by the corporation to receive legal papers that may be served on the corporation. The registered agent should be regularly available at the *registered office* of the corporation. The registered office can be the corporate office, the office of the corporation's attorney, or the office of the registered agent. In most states, the person accepting the position as registered agent must sign a statement that he or she understands the duties and responsibilities of the position.

Bylaws

The *bylaws* are the rules governing the structure and operation of the corporation. Typically, the bylaws will set out rules for the board of directors, officers, and shareholders, and will explain corporate formalities.

Chapter  8

Advantages and Disadvantages of a Corporation

Before forming a corporation, a business owner or prospective business owner should become familiar with the advantages and disadvantages of incorporating.

Advantages

The following are some of the advantages that a corporation has over other forms of businesses, such as sole proprietorships and partnerships.

Limited Liability

The main reason for forming a corporation is to limit the liability of the owners. In a *sole proprietorship* or *partnership*, the owners are personally liable for the debts and liabilities of the business, and in many instances, creditors can go after their personal assets to collect business debts. If a corporation is formed and operated properly, the owners can be protected from all such liability.

For example, if several people are in partnership and one of them makes many extravagant purchases in the name of the partnership, the other partners may be held liable for the full amount of all such purchases. The creditors may be able to take the bank accounts, cars, real estate, and other property of any partner to pay the debts of the partnership. If only one partner has money, he or she may have to pay all of the debts run up by all the other partners.

When doing business as a corporation, the corporation may go bankrupt and the shareholders may lose their initial investment, but the creditors cannot touch the personal assets of the owners.

EXAMPLE: If a person owns a taxi business as a sole proprietor and one of the drivers cause a terrible accident, the owner can be held liable for the full amount of the damages. If the taxi driver was on drugs and killed several people, and the damages amount to millions of dollars more than the insurance coverage, the owner may lose everything he or she owns. On the other hand, if the business is formed as a corporation, only the corporation would be liable, and if there was not enough money, the stockholders still could not be touched personally.

EXAMPLE: There was once a business owner who had hundreds of taxis. He put one or two in each of hundreds of different corporations that he owned. Each corporation only had minimal insurance and when one taxi was involved in an accident, the owner only lost the assets of that corporation.

Alert!

If a corporate officer or shareholder personally does something negligent, signs a debt personally, or guarantees a corporate debt, then the corporation will not protect him or her from the consequences of his or her own act or from the debt. Corporate officers can be held liable by the IRS for payroll taxes that have not been paid, and some states (e.g., New York) hold them liable for unpaid wages.

Perpetual Existence

In all states (except Mississippi), a corporation may have a *perpetual existence*. When a sole proprietor or partner dies, the assets may go to the heirs, but the business no longer exists. If the heirs of the business owner want to continue the business in their own names, they will be considered a new business, even if they are using the assets of the old business. With a partnership, the death of one partner may result in dissolution of the business.

EXAMPLE: If a person dies owning a sole proprietorship, his or her spouse may want to continue the business. That person may inherit all of the assets, but will have to start a new business. This means getting new licenses and tax numbers, re-registering the name, and establishing credit from scratch. With a corporation, the business continues with all of the same licenses, bank accounts, and so on.

EXAMPLE: If one partner dies, a partnership may be forced out of business. The surviving heirs can force the sale of their share of the assets of the partnership, even if the remaining partner needs them to continue the business. If the other partners do not have the money to buy out the heirs, the business may have to be dissolved. With a corporation, the heirs would only inherit stock. With properly drawn documents, the business could continue.

Stock

Stock is the ownership interest in the corporation. The corporation issues shares of its stock to the people or entity who will own the corporation. A corporation can have very few shares of stock or millions of shares. The shares can all represent the same rights in the corporation or there can be different classes of shares with different rights, such as common stock or preferred stock. Stock can be designated with or without *par value*, which is usually the minimum amount paid for stock.

Ease of Transferability

A corporation and all of its assets and accounts may be transferred by the simple assignment of a stock certificate. With a sole proprietorship or partnership, each of the individual assets must be transferred, and the accounts, licenses, and permits must be individually transferred.

EXAMPLE: If a sole proprietorship is sold, the new owner will have to get a new license (if one is required), set up his or her own bank account, and apply for a new federal taxpayer identification number and new state tax account numbers. The title to any vehicles and real estate will have to be put in his or her name, and all open accounts will have to be changed to his or her name. He or she will probably have to submit new credit applications. With a corporation, all of these items remain in the same corporate name.

In some cases, the new owners of a corporation will have to submit personal applications for things such as credit or liquor licenses.

Control

By distributing stock, the owner of a business can share the profits of a business without giving up control.

> **EXAMPLE:** If John wants to give his children some of the profits of his business, he can give them stock and pay dividends to them without giving away any management control. This would not be possible with a partnership or sole proprietorship.

Raising Capital

A corporation may raise capital by selling stock or borrowing money. A corporation does not pay taxes on money it raises by the sale of stock.

> **EXAMPLE:** If a corporation wants to expand, the owners can sell off 10%, 25%, or 45% of the stock and still remain in control of the business. Many individuals considering investing may be more willing to invest if they know they will have a piece of the action in the form of stock.

There are strict rules about the sale of stock, with criminal penalties and triple damages for violators.

Separate Recordkeeping

A corporation is required to keep its bank accounts and records separate from the accounts of its stockholders. A sole proprietor or partnership may mix business and personal accounts, a practice that often causes confusion in recordkeeping and is not recommended.

Tax Advantages

There are several tax advantages that are available only to corporations, such as:

- S corporations may pay less Social Security taxes than LLCs by taking money out as dividends rather than salary;
- corporate owners may be better protected from liability from payroll tax liabilities than LLC owners;
- medical insurance for families may be fully deductible;
- tax-deferred trust can be set up for a retirement plan; and,
- losses are fully deductible for a corporation, whereas an individual must prove there was a profit motive before deducting losses.

Estate Planning

Shares of a company can be distributed more easily with a corporation than with a partnership. Heirs can be given different percentages and control can be limited to the appropriate parties.

Prestige

The name of a corporation often sounds more prestigious than the name of a sole proprietor. John Smith d/b/a Acme Builders sounds like a lone man. Acme Builders, Incorporated sounds as if it might be a large operation. It has been suggested that an individual who is president of a corporation looks more successful than one doing business in his or her own name. The appearance of a business starts with its name.

Separate Credit Rating

A corporation has its own credit rating, which may be better or worse than the shareholders' personal credit ratings. A corporate business can go bankrupt and the shareholder's personal credit will remain unharmed. Conversely, one shareholder's credit may be bad, but the corporation will maintain a good rating. For example, if one shareholder gets a judgment against him or her, this would usually not affect the business of the corporation, whereas it could put an end to a business that was a partnership.

Figure 8.1: **Disadvantages to Incorporating**

Even though there are several advantages to incorporating your business, there are also additional requirements that must be met by the business owner, which some consider disadvantages. The following are some of these requirements.

▶ EXTRA TAX RETURN AND ANNUAL REPORT

A corporation is required to file its own tax return. This is a bit longer and more complicated than the form required for a sole proprietorship or partnership. Additional expenses for the services of an accountant may be required. Typically, a corporation must also file a simple annual report with the state (which lists names and addresses of officers and directors) and pay a fee.

▶ SEPARATE RECORDS

The shareholders of a corporation must be careful to keep their personal business separate from the business of the corporation. The corporation must have its own records, keep minutes of meetings, and keep all corporate money separate from personal money.

▶ EXTRA EXPENSES

There are additional expenses in operating a corporation. People who employ an attorney to form their corporation pay a lot more than people who use this book. Also, in some states, a shareholder may have to pay unemployment or workers' compensation insurance for him- or herself, which he or she would not have to pay as a sole proprietor.

▶ CHECKING ACCOUNTS

Under federal law, checks made out to a corporation cannot be cashed by a shareholder. They must be deposited into a corporate account. Some banks have higher fees just for corporations.

LEGAL REPRESENTATION

Unlike sole proprietors or partners, who can represent themselves in court proceedings, a corporation usually must be represented by an attorney. This may not be necessary in small claims court.

Figure 8.2: **Corporations Compared to LLCs**

Like corporations, limited liability companies (LLCs) offer many benefits over partnerships and sole proprietorships. Whether an LLC or a corporation is better for a small business depends on the type of business.

CORPORATION ADVANTAGES

An S corporation has an advantage over an LLC, which is treated as a disregarded entity, in that the owners of the S corporation can take out some profits without Social Security taxes. However, an LLC can elect to be taxed as an S corporation.

For a large business in which the owners take out salaries of $97,500 or more plus profits (this number adjusts with inflation), there would not be much difference, since the Social Security tax cuts out at about that level. However, for a smaller business, in which an owner could take out a $30,000 salary and $20,000 profit, the extra taxes on the $20,000 would be over $3,000.

If a corporation plans to go public or sell stock to a large group of people, the corporate stock might be easier to sell than membership interests in the LLC.

▶ LLC ADVANTAGES

The most important advantage of an LLC is that in some states, creditors of the owners cannot get the assets of the LLC. With a corporation, creditors of the corporation cannot get the shareholders' assets (if done correctly), but creditors of the shareholders can get their corporate stock.

The other advantages of LLCs are found in certain tax situations. For example, an LLC can make special allocations of profits and losses among members, whereas S corporations cannot. S corporations must have one class of ownership in which profits and losses are allocated according to the percentage ownership. In an LLC, money borrowed by the company can increase the tax basis (and lower the taxes) of the owners, whereas in an S corporation, it does not. Contributing property to set up an LLC is not taxable, even for minority interest owners, whereas for a corporation, regulations only allow it to be tax-free for the contributors who have control of the business. (Internal Revenue Code (I.R.C.), Section 351.)

The owners of an LLC can be foreign persons, other corporations, or any kind of trust, whereas the owners of S corporations cannot. An LLC may have an unlimited number of members, while an S corporation is limited to one hundred.

Alert!

If a corporation does not follow the proper corporate formalities, it may be ignored by a court and the owner may be held personally liable. The formalities include having separate bank accounts, holding meetings, and keeping minutes. When a court ignores a corporate structure and holds the owners liable, it is called *piercing the corporate veil*.

QUICK Tip

When comparing LLCs to corporations, your comparison will typically be to S corporations, which are discussed more specifically in Chapter 9.

Chapter

Types of Corporations

Before forming a corporation, you must make a few choices. Will it be an S or a C corporation? Will it be a closely-held corporation, a professional service corporation, or a nonprofit corporation? The choices you must make are discussed in this chapter, along with the features of the corporation types you have to choose from.

Domestic Corporation or Foreign Corporation

A person wishing to form a corporation must decide whether the corporation will be a domestic corporation or a foreign corporation. A *domestic corporation* is one formed in the state in which it is doing business. A *foreign corporation* is one incorporated in another state or country.

Delaware Corporations

In the past, there was some advantage to incorporating in Delaware, since that state had very liberal laws regarding corporations. Many national corporations are incorporated there. However, in recent years, most states have liberalized their corporation laws—so today, there is no advantage to incorporating in Delaware for most people.

If your state has high corporate fees (such as California), you might save some money by incorporating in Delaware if you are not actively conducting business in your state. If your state has high income taxes (such as New York), you might lower your taxes by having your local corporation pay out all of its profits to a Delaware corporation (which does not pay Delaware income tax if it is not doing business in Delaware).

Nevada Corporations

Nevada has liberalized its corporation laws recently to attract businesses. It allows bearer stock and has other rules that allow more privacy to corporate participants. It also does not share information with the Internal Revenue Service and does not have a state income tax.

Double Incorporation

One way that a Nevada, Delaware, or other corporation can be useful is if your state has high income taxes. By using two corporations, you could transfer your profits to a state that has no income tax.

From a federal tax standpoint there would seldom be an issue, because taxes would have to be paid on the profits no matter which corporation they were in.

From a state tax standpoint there would be a couple of issues. For example, one is whether the Nevada corporation was *doing business* in your state. If the acts of the Nevada corporation are passive enough, it might not even need to register as doing business in your state. For example, if it just loaned money to your corporation, it would not have to register (especially if you happened to go to Las Vegas to sign the loan papers). In most states, merely owning rental real estate does not require a corporation to register.

EXAMPLE: Suppose you were a painting contractor who owned a building and equipment. You could incorporate in your home state as a painting contractor, but put the building and equipment into a Nevada corporation. The Nevada corporation would then lease these to the local corporation. After paying the workers, buying supplies, paying you a salary, and making lease payments to the Nevada corporation, your local company could break even with no taxable profit. The profit would all be in the Nevada corporation, which may not be required to pay taxes in your state.

QUICK Tip

If you are going to set up two corporations for this purpose, you should meet with a local tax specialist to be sure that it is done correctly under your state requirements, as some states have catch-all tax laws that prevent this kind of setup.

Additional Considerations

If you form a corporation in a state other than the one in which your business is located, you will be required to have an agent or an office in that state, and you will have to register as a foreign corporation doing business in your state. This is more expensive and more complicated than incorporating in your own state. Also, if you are sued by someone who is not in your state, he or she can sue you in the state in which you are incorporated, which would probably be more expensive for you than a suit filed in your local court. In some states, your corporation may be required to pay state income tax.

S Corporation or C Corporation

A corporation has a choice of how it wants to be taxed. It can make the election at the beginning of its existence or at the beginning of a new tax year. The choices follow.

S Corporation

Formerly called a "Subchapter S corporation," an *S corporation* pays no income tax and may only be used for small businesses. All of the income or losses of the corporation for the year are passed through to the shareholders, who report them on their individual returns. At the end of each year, the corporation files an *information return*, listing all of its income, expenses, depreciation, etc., and sends each shareholder a notice of his or her share as determined by percentage of stock ownership.

Advantages Using this method avoids double taxation and allows the pass-through of losses and depreciation. For tax purposes, the business is treated as a partnership. Since tax losses are common during the initial years due to start-up costs, many businesses elect S status and switch over to C corporation status in later years. Be aware that once a corporation terminates its S status, there is a waiting period before it can switch back. Typically, S corporations do not have to pay state corporate income tax.

Disadvantages If stockholders are in high income brackets, their share of the profits will be taxed at those rates. Shareholders who do not *materially participate* in the business cannot deduct losses. Some fringe benefits, such as health and life insurance, may not be tax deductible.

Requirements To qualify for S corporation status, the corporation must:

- have no more than one hundred shareholders, none of whom are nonresident aliens or corporations, and all of whom consent to the election (shares owned by a husband and wife jointly are considered owned by one shareholder);
- have only one class of stock;
- not be a member of an *affiliated group* (only individuals, estates, and certain exempt organizations and trusts qualify as affiliated groups);
- generate at least 20% of its income in this country and have no more than 20% of its income from passive sources (e.g., interest, rents, dividends, royalties, and securities transactions); and,
- file Election by a Small Business Corporation (IRS Form 2553) with the IRS before the end of the fifteenth day of the third month of the tax year for which it is to be effective, and be approved by the IRS. Approval is usually routine.

C Corporation

A C *corporation* pays taxes on its net earnings at corporate rates. Salaries of officers, directors, and employees are taxable to them and deductible to the corporation. However, money paid out in dividends is taxed twice. It is taxed at the corporation's rate as part of its profit, and then at the individual stockholders' rates as income, when distributed by the corporation to them.

Advantages If taxpayers are in a higher tax bracket than the corporation and the money will be left in the company for expansion, taxes are saved. Fringe benefits, such as health, accident, and life insurance, are deductible expenses.

Disadvantages Double taxation of dividends by the federal government can be a big disadvantage. Also, most states have an income tax that only applies to C corporations and applies to all income over a certain amount.

Requirements There are no requirements for being a C as opposed to an S corporation.

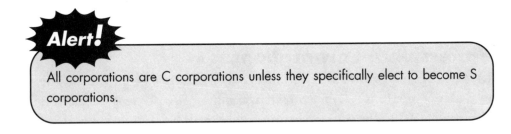

Alert!

All corporations are C corporations unless they specifically elect to become S corporations.

Many small business owners take all profits out as salaries to avoid double taxation and state income tax. However, there are rules requiring that salaries be reasonable. If a stockholder's salary is deemed to be too high relative to his or her job, the salary may be considered to be partially a dividend and subject to double taxation.

Closely-Held Corporation

A *closely-held corporation* election is beneficial for many small businesses. Its purpose is to place restrictions on the transferability of stock. Often, it obligates a shareholder to offer to the corporation or the shareholders the opportunity to purchase the stock before offering it to any outside purchaser. If the corporation and shareholders reject the offer, they typically must still consent to who the transferee (buyer) of the shares will be.

If you elect to have these restrictions, they should be included in the bylaws and printed on the certificates—and in many states, they must be included in the articles of incorporation.

Professional Corporations

Under the laws of most states, certain types of services can only be rendered by a corporation if it is a *professional association* (P.A.) or *professional service corporation* (P.C.). These include such professionals as attorneys, physicians, certified public accountants, veterinarians, architects, life insurance agents, and chiropractors. For simplicity, these will be referred to as *professional service corporations*. A professional service corporation typically has specific rules under the state incorporation statutes.

Purpose

A professional service corporation must usually have one specific purpose spelled out in the articles of incorporation, and that purpose must be to practice a specific profession. It may not engage in any other business, but it may invest its funds in real estate, stocks, bonds, mortgages, or other types of investments. A professional service corporation may change its purpose to another legal purpose, but it will then no longer be a professional service corporation.

Name

In most states, the name of a professional service corporation must contain the words "chartered," "professional association," or "professional corporation," or the abbreviations "P.A." or "P.C." Typically, it may not use the words "company," "corporation," "incorporated," or any abbreviation of these.

Shareholders

According to the law in most states, only persons licensed to practice a profession may be shareholders of a professional service corporation engaged in that practice. A shareholder who loses the right to practice must immediately sever all employment with, and financial interests in, such a corporation. If such a shareholder does not sever these ties, the corporation may be dissolved by the state. No shareholder may enter into a voting trust or other similar arrangement with anyone.

Merger

A professional service corporation may not merge with any other corporation except a professional service corporation that is licensed to perform the same type of service.

Requirements

Most states have very specific requirements for the formation of professional service corporations. They often require specific language in the articles, charter, or bylaws. For this type of corporation, you should consult an attorney.

Nonprofit Corporations

Nonprofit corporations are usually used for social clubs, churches, and charities, and are beyond the scope of this book. While they are similar to for-profit corporations in many aspects, such as limited liability and the required formalities, there are additional state and federal requirements that must be met.

In some cases, a business can be formed as a nonprofit corporation. It would not be allowed to distribute profits to its founders, but it could pay substantial salaries and enjoy numerous tax advantages.

Chapter  10

Start-Up Procedures

The steps necessary to legally establish your corporation are not difficult, but still need to be followed closely. Such preliminary things as checking on available corporate names must be done, as well as filing the required paperwork and acquiring taxpayer information. This chapter takes you through these steps.

Name Search
The first thing to do before starting a corporation is to thoroughly check out the name you wish to use, to be sure it is not already being used by someone else. Many businesses have been forced to stop using their name after spending thousands of dollars promoting it.

Corporate Records

The first place to check is your secretary of state's office to see if the name has already been used by another corporation in your state. To do this, you can write or call their office. In some states, you can access your state's corporate records through the Internet and conduct your own search of all current and dissolved corporations. If your state's records are not listed or have changed, you may be able to access them at www.findlaw.com/11stategov/index.html.

Fictitious Names

Besides checking corporate names, you should check if another business is using the name you want as a *fictitious name*. In some states these are registered with each county, and in others they are registered with the secretary of state. Some states that register the names with the secretary of state can be searched over the Internet as described above.

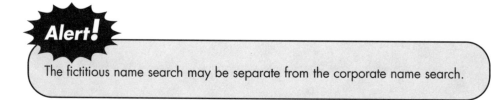

Alert! The fictitious name search may be separate from the corporate name search.

Business Listings

Since some businesses neglect to properly register their name (yet still may have superior rights to the name), you should also check phone books and business directories. Many libraries have phone books from around the country as well as directories of trade names.

Yellow Page Listings

If you have a computer with Internet access, you can search every Yellow Page listing for free. Just search for "yellow pages" with any Web search engine (e.g., Google, Yahoo, WebCrawler, Lycos, etc.). You can select a state and enter your business name. It will tell you if any other companies are listed with that name. One site that allows you to search all states at once is **www.switchboard.com**.

Trademark Search

To be sure that you are not violating a registered trademark, you should have a search done of the records of the *United States Patent and Trademark Office* (PTO). In the past, this required a visit to their offices or the hiring of a search firm for over a hundred dollars. Recently, the PTO put its trademark records online, so now you can search them through the PTO website. Go to **www.uspto.gov** and click on the "Trademarks" button. Click on "Search Trademarks," which will take you to the *Trademark Electronic Search System* (TESS). For a more thorough search, you can have the search done through a firm.

Figure 10.1: **Firms that Conduct Trademark Searches**

**Government Liaison
Services, Inc.**
200 North Glebe Road
Suite 321
Arlington, VA 22203
800-642-6564
703-524-8200
www.trademarkinfo.com

XL Corporate Service
62 White Street
New York, NY 10013
800-529-6278
212-431-5000

Thomson & Thomson
500 Victory Road
North Quincy, MA 02171
800-692-8833
www.thomson-thomson.com

Name Reservation

It is possible to reserve a name for a corporation for a certain period of time by filing a reservation form and paying the appropriate fee. However, this is usually pointless because it is just as easy to file the articles as it is to reserve the name. One possible reason for reserving a name would be to hold it while waiting for a trademark name search to arrive.

Fictitious Names

Since a corporation has a legal name, it does not need a fictitious name, but a corporation may operate under a fictitious or assumed name just as an individual can. This is done when a corporation wants to operate several businesses under different names or if the business name is not available as a corporate name. Fictitious names are either registered in each county or are registered statewide with the secretary of state. However, registering a fictitious name does not give the registrant any rights to the name. While corporate names are carefully checked by the secretary of state and disallowed if they are similar to others, in many states fictitious names are filed without checking and any number of people may register the same name. The cost of registering a fictitious name varies. Application forms and instructions can be obtained from your local courthouse, appropriate county office, or secretary of state's office.

QUICK Tip

When a fictitious name is used by a corporation, the corporate name should also be used. This is because if the public does not see that they are dealing with a corporation, they may be able to pierce the corporate veil and sue the stockholders individually. Thus, all signs, business cards, etc., should list the names in one of the following ways:

Smith Enterprises, Inc. d/b/a Internet Resources

or

Internet Resources, a division of Smith Enterprises, Inc.

Similar Names

Sometimes it seems as if every good name is taken. However, a name can often be modified slightly or used on a different type of product or service. Try different variations if your favorite is taken. Another possibility is to give the corporation one name and then do business under a fictitious name.

> **EXAMPLE:** If you want to use the name "Flowers by Freida" in Pensacola and there is already a "Flowers by Freida, Inc." in Miami, you might incorporate under the name "Freida Jones, Inc." and then register the corporation as doing business under the fictitious name "Flowers by Freida." Unless "Flowers by Freida, Inc." has registered a trademark for the name either in Florida or nationally, you will probably be able to use the name.

Alert!

You should realize that you might run into complications later, especially if you decide to expand into other areas of the state or other states. One protection available would be to register the name used on your goods or services as a trademark. This would give you exclusive use of the name anywhere that it was not already being used.

Forbidden Names

A corporation may not use certain words in its name if there would be a likelihood of confusion. There are state and federal laws that control the use of these words. In most cases, your application will be rejected if you use a forbidden word.

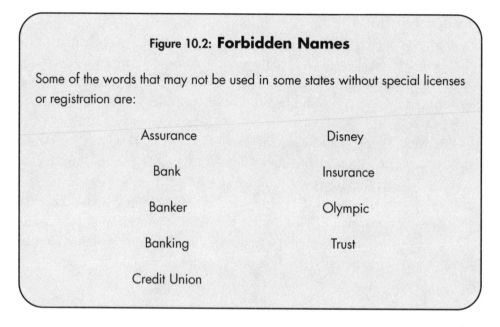

Figure 10.2: Forbidden Names

Some of the words that may not be used in some states without special licenses or registration are:

Assurance	Disney
Bank	Insurance
Banker	Olympic
Banking	Trust
Credit Union	

If you use a word that is forbidden, your papers will most likely be returned. You may wish to call the corporate registrar to ask if the name you plan to use is allowed.

Trademarks

The name of a business may not be registered as a *trademark*, but a name used on goods or to sell services may be registered, and such registration will grant the holder exclusive rights to use that name except in areas where someone else has used the name. A trademark may be registered both in your state and in the United States Patent and Trademark Office.

Each trademark is registered for a certain *class* of goods. You may usually register the name "Kapow" chewing gum even if someone has registered the name "Kapow" for use on shoes. One exception to this rule is if the name is so well known that your use would cause confusion. For example, you could not use "Coca-Cola" as a brand of shoes, because people are so familiar with the Coca-Cola company that they might think the company started a line of shoes. If you want to register the mark for several types of goods or services, you must register it for each different class into which the goods or services fall, and pay a separate fee for each category.

For protection within each state, the mark may be registered with each state's appropriate department handling trademarks. The cost varies from state to state. Application forms and instructions can be obtained through the same department.

For protection across the entire United States, the mark can be registered with the United States Patent and Trademark Office. At the time of publication of this book, the fee is $375. The procedure for federal registration is more complicated than state registration and is beyond the scope of this book. Visit the PTO website at **www.uspto.gov** for more information.

Articles of Incorporation

To create a corporation, a document must be filed with the state agency that keeps corporate records, which in most states is the secretary of state. In most states, this document is called the *articles of incorporation*. However, in some states, it may be called the *certificate of incorporation*, the *articles of association*, or the *charter*. This document is referred to as the articles of incorporation throughout this book. Some corporations have long, elaborate articles that describe numerous powers and functions, but most of this is unnecessary. The powers of corporations are explained in state law and do not have to be repeated. Short articles are just as legal and allow more flexibility.

Typically, state law requires only a minimum amount of detail be included in the articles of incorporation. Some things, such as the purpose of the corporation, regulations for the operation of the corporation, and a par value of the stock, may be explained in the articles of incorporation. This is not advisable unless required, since any changes would necessitate the complicated process of amending the articles. It is better to explain these terms in the bylaws. The matters typically required to be contained in the articles and a few of the optional provisions follow.

Name of the Corporation

Most states require that the corporation name contain one of the following six words:

- Incorporated
- Inc.
- Corporation
- Corp.
- Company
- Co.

The reason for the requirement is so that persons dealing with the business will be on notice that it is a corporation. This is important in protecting the shareholders from liability.

Address of the Corporation

The street address of the principal office and the mailing address of the corporation must be provided.

The Number of Shares of Stock the Corporation is Authorized to Issue

The number of shares of stock the corporation is authorized to issue is usually an even number, such as 100, 1,000, or 1,000,000.

In some cases it may be advantageous to issue different *classes* of stock—such as common and preferred, or voting and nonvoting—but such matters should be discussed with an attorney or accountant.

If there are different classes of stock, then the articles of incorporation must contain a designation of the classes and a statement of the preferences, limitations, and relative rights of each class. In addition, if there are to be any preferred or special shares issued in *series*, then the articles must explain the relative rights and preferences, and any authority of the board of directors to establish preferences. Any preemptive rights must also be explained.

This book explains how to form a corporation with one class of stock. It is usually advisable to authorize double or quadruple the amount of stock that will be initially issued. The unissued stock can be issued later if more capital is contributed by a shareholder or by a new member of the business.

One important point to keep in mind when issuing stock relates to par value. *Par value* is the total number of shares that a corporation may issue under its articles, divided by the total initial investment in the corporation.

Par value is not always the actual value of the stock because a corporation's net worth may play a role. When issuing stock, the full par value must be paid for in shares. If this is not done, then the shareholder can later be held liable for the full par value.

The Name of the Registered Agent and the Address of the Registered Office, Along with the Agent's Acceptance

Each corporation must have a *registered agent* and a *registered office.* The registered office can be the business office of the corporation if the registered agent works out of that office, it can be the office of another individual who is the registered agent (such as an attorney), or it may be a corporate registered agent's office. Technically, it may not be a residence, unless that address is also a business office of the corporation. Penalty for failure to comply can be the inability to maintain a lawsuit and a possible fine.

The Name and Address of the Incorporator of the Corporation

The incorporator may be any person, even if that person has no future interest in the corporation. There are companies in state capitals that will, on a moment's notice, have someone run over to the secretary of state to file corporate articles that are later assigned to the real parties in interest. However, in some states, those who maintain deposits of funds with the secretary of state are allowed to file articles by facsimile, so there is less need to run these days.

Duration

In most states, the duration of the corporation need not be mentioned if it is to be *perpetual.* If not, the duration must be specified in the articles.

Effective Date

A specific effective date may be in the articles, but is not required. Articles are effective upon filing. If an effective date is specified, state law varies as to the time before or after the filing in which the articles of incorporation are effective.

Execution

The articles of incorporation must be signed by the incorporator and dated. Typically, the registered agent must sign a statement accepting his or her duties as such. This is sometimes done as a separate form or sometimes on the same form as the articles.

Forms

The articles of incorporation need not be on any certain form. They can be typed on blank paper or can be on a fill-in-the-blank form. Some states have their own incorporation forms, which you can get by mail or over the Internet.

The articles of incorporation must be filed with the secretary of state and the filing fee must be paid. If you wish to receive a certified copy of the articles, the cost is additional. In many states this is an unnecessary expense, since a certified copy is rarely, if ever, needed. Ask your bank if it will require a certified copy. Usually, the better alternative is to enclose a photocopy along with the articles and ask that it be stamped with the filing date and returned.

QUICK Tip

In most states, the return time for the articles is usually a week or two. If there is a need to have them back quickly, you might be able to send them and have them returned by a courier such as FedEx, Airborne Express, or UPS, with prepaid return. Call your secretary of state for details.

Shareholder Agreement

When there are two or more shareholders in a corporation, they should consider drawing up a shareholder agreement. This document explains what is to happen in the event of a disagreement between the parties. In closely-held corporations, the minority shareholders have a risk of being locked into a long-term enterprise with little or no way to withdraw their capital. Even family corporations should consider a *shareholder agreement*, since it could settle some issues without the expense of litigation.

A shareholder agreement is a fairly complicated document and should be drawn up by an attorney. This may be costly, but the expense should be weighed against the costs of lengthy litigation should the parties break up.

Some of the issues that are usually included in a shareholder agreement are discussed below, and a simple blank shareholder agreement form can be read in Figure 10.3 on page 108. This might suit your needs while your corporation is small. Review it as your company grows to be sure it still fits your needs.

When drawing up a shareholder agreement, you will consider your options during the expansion of your company, but be sure to also consider the possibility of negative events, such as bankruptcy or death of a participant. These are the times when a shareholder agreement is most needed.

Rights of Minority

The biggest risk in a small corporation with unequal ownership is that an owner of a minority interest will be shut out of making decisions. Unless some rights are spelled out in a shareholder agreement, any shareholder with less than 50% interest risks having his or her investment tied up indefinitely. Many of the clauses in a shareholder agreement address various rights (such as salary and withdrawal) of shareholders with a minority interest.

Supermajority Vote or Unanimous Consent

In order to allow shareholders with minority interests to have a say in major changes in the corporation, you can require unanimous consent or more than simple majority vote (*supermajority*) on such issues. One danger to keep in mind is that requiring unanimous consent can allow one disgruntled shareholder to sabotage the efforts of the majority.

QUICK Tip

If the majority wants to sell the company, you would not want one shareholder with 10% interest to kill the deal. You should seek an agreement that can balance the rights of the majority and the minority. If a 10% owner is the only one who does not want to sell, then he or she can be given the right to buy out the other 90%.

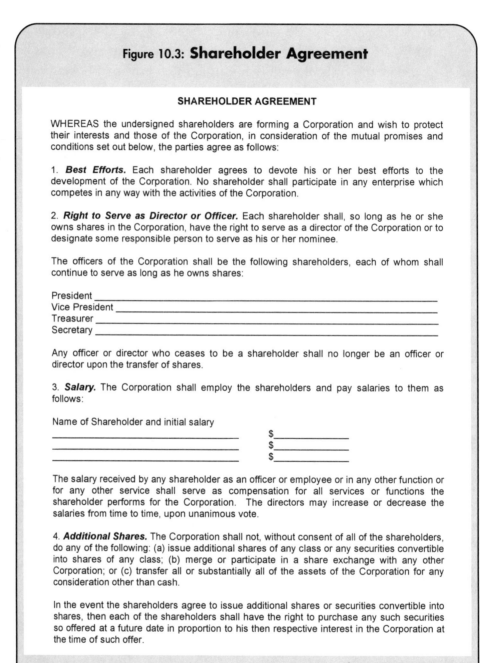

Figure 10.3: Shareholder Agreement

SHAREHOLDER AGREEMENT

WHEREAS the undersigned shareholders are forming a Corporation and wish to protect their interests and those of the Corporation, in consideration of the mutual promises and conditions set out below, the parties agree as follows:

1. **Best Efforts.** Each shareholder agrees to devote his or her best efforts to the development of the Corporation. No shareholder shall participate in any enterprise which competes in any way with the activities of the Corporation.

2. **Right to Serve as Director or Officer.** Each shareholder shall, so long as he or she owns shares in the Corporation, have the right to serve as a director of the Corporation or to designate some responsible person to serve as his or her nominee.

The officers of the Corporation shall be the following shareholders, each of whom shall continue to serve as long as he owns shares:

President _____
Vice President _____
Treasurer _____
Secretary _____

Any officer or director who ceases to be a shareholder shall no longer be an officer or director upon the transfer of shares.

3. **Salary.** The Corporation shall employ the shareholders and pay salaries to them as follows:

Name of Shareholder and initial salary

_____ $_____
_____ $_____
_____ $_____

The salary received by any shareholder as an officer or employee or in any other function or for any other service shall serve as compensation for all services or functions the shareholder performs for the Corporation. The directors may increase or decrease the salaries from time to time, upon unanimous vote.

4. **Additional Shares.** The Corporation shall not, without consent of all of the shareholders, do any of the following: (a) issue additional shares of any class or any securities convertible into shares of any class; (b) merge or participate in a share exchange with any other Corporation; or (c) transfer all or substantially all of the assets of the Corporation for any consideration other than cash.

In the event the shareholders agree to issue additional shares or securities convertible into shares, then each of the shareholders shall have the right to purchase any such securities so offered at a future date in proportion to his then respective interest in the Corporation at the time of such offer.

5. ***Transfer of Shares.*** No shares shall be transferred in any manner or by any means except upon unanimous consent of the shareholders. If a proposed sale is not agreed to by unanimous consent, a shareholder may resign from his or her positions with the corporation and be bought out by the corporation as provided below.

6. ***Buyout.*** Upon the death, resignation, adjudication of incompetency, or bankruptcy by any shareholder, or the transfer, agreement to transfer, or attachment of any shares, the Corporation shall purchase all of the shares of the shareholder so affected at the value of shares described below. Payment by the corporation for such buyout shall be within thirty days of the determination of value and the transferring shareholder shall execute all documents necessary to transfer his or her shares.

7. ***Value of Shares.*** The parties agree that upon execution of this agreement the value of each share of stock is $_____. This value shall be reviewed and updated once each year and at any time that a sale of shares is contemplated. New value shall be set by a unanimous vote of the shareholders. If the shareholders cannot agree, then the corporation's accountant shall be asked to set a value. If any shareholder disagrees with the corporation's accountant's value, he or she may get the value of another accountant. If the two accountants cannot agree to an acceptable value, they shall choose a third accountant to set the final value.

8. ***S Corporation Status.*** If the Corporation is an S corporation and if it reasonably determines that any proposed transferee is not eligible as a shareholder of a Subchapter S Corporation or that such transfer would cause the Corporation to lose its qualification as a Subchapter S Corporation, then the Corporation may so notify the shareholder of that determination and thereby forbid the consummation of the transfer.

9. ***Endorsement.*** The certificates for shares of the Corporation shall be endorsed as follows: "The shares represented by this certificate are subject to and are transferable only on compliance with a Shareholders Agreement a copy of which is on file in the office of the Secretary of the Corporation."

10. ***Formalities.*** Whenever under this Agreement notice is required to be given, it shall be given in writing served in person or by certified or registered mail, return receipt requested, to the address of the shareholder listed in the stock ledger of the corporation, and it shall be deemed to have been given upon personal delivery or on the date notice is posted.

11. ***Termination.*** This Agreement shall terminate and all rights and obligations hereunder shall cease upon the happening of any one of the following events:

(a) The adjudication of the Corporation as bankrupt, the execution by it of any assignment for the benefit of creditors, or the appointment of a receiver for the Corporation.

(b) The voluntary or involuntary dissolution of the Corporation.

(c) By a written Agreement signed by all the shareholders to terminate this Agreement.

12. ***Entire Agreement.*** This Agreement embodies the entire representations, Agreements and conditions in relation to the subject matter hereof and no representations,

understandings or Agreements, oral or otherwise, in relation thereto exist between the parties except as herein expressly set forth. The Agreement may not be amended or terminated orally but only as expressly provided herein or by an instrument in writing duly executed by the parties hereto.

13. *Heirs and Assigns.* This Agreement and the various rights and obligations arising under it shall inure to the benefit of and be binding upon the parties hereto and their respective heirs, successors and assigns.

14. **Severability.** The invalidity or unenforceability of any term or provision of this Agreement or the non-application of such term or provision to any person or circumstance shall not impair or affect the remainder of this Agreement, and its application to other persons and circumstances and the remaining terms and provisions hereof shall not be invalidated but shall remain in full force and effect.

15. *Gender.* Whenever in this Agreement any pronoun is used in reference to any shareholder, purchaser or other person or entity, natural or otherwise, the singular shall include the plural, and the masculine shall include the feminine or the neuter, as required by context.

16. *Arbitration.* All disputes between shareholders or between the corporation and a shareholder shall be settled by arbitration and the parties hereto specifically waive they rights to bring action in any court, except to enforce an arbitration decision.

17. *Choice of Law.* This Agreement shall be governed by and construed in accordance with the laws of the State of _____.

IN WITNESS WHEREOF, the parties hereto have executed this Agreement the date and place first above mentioned.

_____ [Name of Corporation]

By: _____,
                President

_____ Shareholder

_____ Shareholder

_____ Shareholder

_____ Shareholder

Devoting Best Efforts

One problem that sometimes comes up in the life of a corporation is that one shareholder loses interest and no longer contributes the time that was originally expected. Another problem may arise when a shareholder becomes a part of a competing enterprise. To avoid disagreements, you should spell out what is expected of each shareholder. You could spell out how many hours a week each person is expected to work, or you could just have a general agreement that each shareholder will devote his or her best efforts to the company.

Right to Serve as Director

A very effective protection for minority shareholders is the right of each to serve as a director. This enables them to take part in directors' meetings without being elected and to stay informed of activities of the corporation. However, being a director does not guarantee a right to control decisions.

Salary

If there is a chance that some of the shareholders will later vote themselves higher salaries than others, you can include an agreement as to what the salaries will be and include a requirement that any change must be agreed to by everyone or by more than a simple majority.

Nominating Officers and Employees

One common provision in a shareholder agreement is to agree on what office will be held by each shareholder. Any change could require unanimous consent or a supermajority vote. However, be sure to provide for the possibility that someone may become unable or unwilling to do the job.

Compulsory Buyout

A way to end a dispute between shareholders is to provide for a *compulsory buyout*. This can be *open-ended*, in which either party can buy out the other, or it can be *specific*, in which one person's shares are subject to a buyout. A formula for determining the buyout price should be in the agreement, to avoid disagreements later.

Transfer of Shares

Most small corporations limit the ability of shareholders to sell their shares. This protects the corporation from violations of securities laws and from persons whom they might not want as shareholders. A limitation on the ability to sell shares is usually combined with a buyout plan.

Additional Shares

To maintain a balance of power among the shareholders, it is important to have provisions covering the issuance of new shares or a merger with another corporation. Besides a clause that provides a majority or unanimous consent for decisions concerning these events, a provision to issue new shares on a *pro rata* basis can solve some situations.

Transfer of Substantial Assets

To protect the shareholders' value, a clause should be added that any transfer of substantial assets for any consideration other than cash is not allowed.

Endorsement

An *endorsement* on the shares informs a potential transferee about the circumstance that the shares are subject to certain restrictions concerning their transfer. It warns the transferee and betters the chances of the corporation in case of a lawsuit due to a transfer not being in accordance with the provisions of the shareholder agreement.

Formalities

To avoid any misunderstanding, the formalities as to how the shareholder agreement should be complied with can be included.

Arbitration

Because going to court is so expensive and can take years, it is a good idea to put an *arbitration* clause in your agreement. Arbitrators, who mediate legal disagreements and issue decisions on them, are often lawyers or former judges, so you get a decision similar to what you would have gotten in court, without the expense or delay.

Boilerplate Language

Most shareholder agreements contain standard legal *boilerplate* language, such as *entire agreement* (there are no verbal additions to this agreement), *severability* (if one clause is invalid that would not be reason to throw out the entire agreement), and *choice of law* (which state's laws will be used to interpret the agreement).

Organizational Paperwork

Every corporation must have *bylaws* and must maintain a set of *minutes* of its meetings. The bylaws must be adopted at the first meeting, and the first minutes of the corporation will record the proceedings of the organizational meeting.

Waiver of Notice

Before any meeting of the incorporators, board of directors, or shareholders can be held, formal notice must be given to the parties of the meeting. Since small corporations often need to have meetings on short notice and do not want to be bothered with formal notices, it is customary to have all parties sign written waivers of notice.

Bylaws

The *bylaws* are the rules for organization and operation of the corporation. They are required by state law. Figure 10.4 is a blank sample form of bylaws for a simple corporation. To complete it, fill in the name and state of the corporation, the city of the main office of the corporation, the proposed date of the annual meeting (this can vary each year, as needed), and the number of directors to be on the board.

Minutes

As part of the formal requirements of operating a corporation, *minutes* must be kept of the meetings of shareholders and the board of directors. Usually only one meeting of each is required each year, unless there is some special need for a meeting in the interim (such as the resignation of an officer). The first minutes will be the minutes of the organizational meeting of the corporation. At this meeting, the officers and directors are elected; the bylaws, corporate seal, and stock certificates are adopted; and, other organizational decisions are made.

Resolutions

When the board of directors or shareholders make major decisions, it is usually done in the form of a *resolution*. At the organizational meeting, some important resolutions that may be passed are choosing a bank and adopting S corporation status.

Tax Forms

Prior to opening a bank account, the corporation must obtain an *employer identification number* (EIN), which is the corporate equivalent of a Social Security number. This is done by filing an Application for Employer Identification Number (IRS Form SS-4) with the Internal Revenue Service.

If you mail this form in, it can take weeks, but you can get your number within a day by phoning the number in the instructions. You will need to have the form completed and in front of you when you call, and you may need to fax the sheet to them. The phone number to obtain the EIN is 800-829-4933.

You may also file online. Go to **www.irs.gov** and search the term "SS-4 online." Follow the instructions for completing the form as you would for a written application. You will receive your EIN shortly thereafter electronically, with a paper receipt mailed to you within two weeks.

When you apply for this number, you will probably be put on the mailing list for other corporate tax forms. If you do not receive these, you should call your local IRS office and request the forms for new businesses. These include *Circular E* (which explains the taxes due), *W-4 forms* for each employee, tax deposit coupons, and *Form 941* quarterly return for withholding.

IRS Form 2553

If your corporation is to be taxed as an S corporation, you must file an Election by a Small Business Corporation (IRS Form 2553) with the IRS within seventy-five days of incorporation. As a practical matter, you should sign and file this at your organizational meeting; otherwise, you may forget.

Figure 10.4: **Bylaws**

BYLAWS OF

_____

A _____ CORPORATION

ARTICLE I—OFFICES

The principal office of the Corporation shall be located in the City of _____ _____ and the State of _____. The Corporation may also maintain offices at such other places as the Board of Directors may, from time to time, determine.

ARTICLE II—SHAREHOLDERS

Section 1—Annual Meetings: The annual meeting of the shareholders of the Corporation shall be held each year on _____ at _____ m. at the principal office of the Corporation or at such other places, within or without the State of _____, as the Board may authorize, for the purpose of electing directors, and transacting such other business as may properly come before the meeting.

Section 2—Special Meetings: Special meetings of the shareholders may be called at any time by the Board, the President, or by the holders of twenty-five percent (25%) of the shares then outstanding and entitled to vote.

Section 3—Place of Meetings: All meetings of shareholders shall be held at the principal office of the Corporation, or at such other places as the board shall designate in the notice of such meetings.

Section 4—Notice of Meetings: Written or printed notice stating the place, day, and hour of the meeting and, in the case of a special meeting, the purpose of the meeting, shall be delivered personally or by mail not less than ten days, nor more than sixty days, before the date of the meeting. Notice shall be given to each Member of record entitled to vote at the meeting. If mailed, such notice shall be deemed to have been delivered when deposited in the United States Mail with postage paid and addressed to the Member at his or her address as it appears on the records of the Corporation.

Section 5—Waiver of Notice: A written waiver of notice signed by a Member, whether before or after a meeting, shall be equivalent to the giving of such notice. Attendance of a Member at a meeting shall constitute a waiver of notice of such meeting, except when the Member attends for the express purpose of objecting, at the beginning of the meeting, to the transaction of any business because the meeting is not lawfully called or convened.

Section 6—Quorum: Except as otherwise provided by Statute, or the Articles of Incorporation, at all meetings of shareholders of the Corporation, the presence at the commencement of such meetings in person or by proxy of shareholders of record holding a majority of the total number of shares of the Corporation then issued and outstanding and entitled to vote, but in no event less than one-third of the shares entitled to vote at the meeting, shall constitute a quorum for the transaction of any business. If any shareholder leaves after the commencement of a meeting, this shall have no effect on the existence of a quorum, after a quorum has been established at such meeting.

Despite the absence of a quorum at any annual or special meeting of shareholders, the shareholders, by a majority of the votes cast by the holders of shares entitled to vote thereon, may adjourn the meeting. At any such adjourned meeting at which a quorum is present, any business may be transacted at the meeting as originally called as if a quorum had been present.

Section 7—Voting: Except as otherwise provided by Statute or by the Articles of Incorporation, any corporate action, other than the election of directors, to be taken by vote of the shareholders, shall be authorized by a majority of votes cast at a meeting of shareholders by the holders of shares entitled to vote thereon.

Except as otherwise provided by Statute or by the Articles of Incorporation, at each meeting of shareholders, each holder of record of stock of the Corporation entitled to vote thereat, shall be entitled to one vote for each share of stock registered in his or her name on the stock transfer books of the corporation.

Each shareholder entitled to vote may do so by proxy; provided, however, that the instrument authorizing such proxy to act shall have been executed in writing by the shareholder him- or herself. No proxy shall be valid after the expiration of eleven months from the date of its execution, unless the person executing it shall have specified therein, the length of time it is to continue in force. Such instrument shall be exhibited to the Secretary at the meeting and shall be filed with the records of the corporation.

Any resolution in writing, signed by all of the shareholders entitled to vote thereon, shall be and constitute action by such shareholders to the effect therein expressed, with the same force and effect as if the same had been duly passed by unanimous vote at a duly called meeting of shareholders and such resolution so signed shall be inserted in the Minute Book of the Corporation under its proper date.

ARTICLE III—BOARD OF DIRECTORS

Section 1—Number, Election and Term of Office: The number of the directors of the Corporation shall be (____). This number may be increased or decreased by the amendment of these bylaws by the Board but shall in no case be less than _____ director(s). The members of the Board, who need not be shareholders, shall be elected by a majority of the votes cast at a meeting of shareholders entitled to vote in the election. Each director shall hold office until the annual meeting of the shareholders next succeeding his election, and until his successor is elected and qualified, or until his prior death, resignation or removal.

Section 2—Vacancies: Any vacancy in the Board shall be filled for the unexpired portion of the term by a majority vote of the remaining directors, though less than a quorum, at any regular meeting or special meeting of the Board called for that purpose. Any such director so elected may be replaced by the shareholders at a regular or special meeting of shareholders.

Section 3—Duties and Powers: The Board shall be responsible for the control and management of the affairs, property and interests of the Corporation, and may exercise all powers of the Corporation, except as limited by statute.

Section 4—Annual Meetings: An annual meeting of the Board shall be held immediately following the annual meeting of the shareholders, at the place of such annual meeting of shareholders. The Board from time to time, may provide by resolution for the holding of other meetings of the Board, and may fix the time and place thereof.

Section 5—Special Meetings: Special meetings of the Board shall be held whenever called by the President or by one of the directors, at such time and place as may be specified in the respective notice or waivers of notice thereof.

Section 6—Notice and Waiver: Notice of any special meeting shall be given at least five days prior thereto by written notice delivered personally, by mail, or by telegram to each Director at his or her address. If mailed, such notice shall be deemed to be delivered when deposited in the United States Mail with postage prepaid. If notice is given by telegram, such notice shall be deemed to be delivered when the telegram is delivered to the telegraph company.

Any Director may waive notice of any meeting, either before, at, or after such meeting, by signing a waiver of notice. The attendance of a Director at a meeting shall constitute a waiver of notice of such meeting and a waiver of any and all objections to the place of such meeting, or the manner in which it has been called or convened, except when a Director states at the beginning of the meeting any objection to the transaction of business because the meeting is not lawfully called or convened.

Section 7—Chairman: The Board may, at its discretion, elect a Chairman. At all meetings of the Board, the Chairman of the Board, if any and if present, shall preside. If there is no Chairman, or he or she is absent, then the President shall preside, and in his or her absence, a Chairman chosen by the directors shall preside.

Section 8—Quorum and Adjournments: At all meetings of the Board, the presence of a majority of the entire Board shall be necessary and sufficient to constitute a quorum for the transaction of business, except as otherwise provided by law, by the Articles of Incorporation, or by these bylaws. A majority of the directors present at the time and place of any regular or special meeting, although less than a quorum, may adjourn the same from time to time without notice, until a quorum shall be present.

Section 9—Board Action: At all meetings of the Board, each director present shall have one vote, irrespective of the number of shares of stock, if any, which he may hold. Except as otherwise provided by Statute, the action of a majority of the directors present at any meeting at which a quorum is present shall be the act of the Board. Any action authorized, in writing, by all of the Directors entitled to vote thereon and filed with the minutes of the Corporation shall be the act of the Board with the same force and effect as if the same had been passed by unanimous vote at a duly called meeting of the Board. Any action taken by the Board may be taken without a meeting if agreed to in writing by all members before or after the action is taken and if a record of such action is filed in the minute book.

Section 10—Telephone Meetings: Directors may participate in meetings of the Board through use of a telephone if such can be arranged so that all Board members can hear all other members. The use of a telephone for participation shall constitute presence in person.

Section 11—Resignation and Removal: Any director may resign at any time by giving written notice to another Board member, the President or the Secretary of the Corporation. Unless otherwise specified in such written notice, such resignation shall take effect upon receipt thereof by the Board or by such officer, and the acceptance of such resignation shall not be necessary to make it effective. Any director may be removed with or without cause at any time by the affirmative vote of shareholders holding of record in the aggregate at least a majority of the outstanding shares of the Corporation at a special meeting of the shareholders called for that purpose, and may be removed for cause by action of the Board.

Section 12—Compensation: No stated salary shall be paid to directors, as such for their services, but by resolution of the Board a fixed sum and/or expenses of attendance, if any, may be allowed for attendance at each regular or special meeting of the Board. Nothing herein contained shall be construed to preclude any director from serving the Corporation in any other capacity and receiving compensation therefor.

ARTICLE IV—OFFICERS

Section 1—Number, Qualification, Election and Term: The officers of the Corporation shall consist of a President, a Secretary, a Treasurer, and such other officers, as the Board may from time to time deem advisable. Any officer may be, but is not required to be, a director of the Corporation. The officers of the Corporation shall be elected by the Board at the regular annual meeting of the Board. Each officer shall hold office until the annual meeting of the Board next succeeding his or her election, and until his or her successor shall have been elected and qualified, or until his or her death, resignation, or removal.

Section 2—Resignation and Removal: Any officer may resign at any time by giving written notice of such resignation to the President or the Secretary of the Corporation or to a member of the Board. Unless otherwise specified in such written notice, such resignation shall take effect upon receipt thereof by the Board member or by such officer, and the acceptance of such resignation shall not be necessary to make it effective. Any officer may be removed, either with or without cause, and a successor elected by a majority vote of the Board at any time.

Section 3—Vacancies: A vacancy in any office may at any time be filled for the unexpired portion of the term by a majority vote of the Board.

Section 4—Duties of Officers: Officers of the Corporation shall, unless otherwise provided by the Board, each have such powers and duties as generally pertain to their respective offices as well as such powers and duties as may from time to time be specifically decided by the Board. The President shall be the chief executive officer of the Corporation.

Section 5—Compensation: The officers of the Corporation shall be entitled to such compensation as the Board shall from time to time determine.

Section 6—Delegation of Duties: In the absence or disability of any Officer of the Corporation or for any other reason deemed sufficient by the Board of Directors, the Board may delegate his or her powers or duties to any other Officer or to any other Director.

Section 7—Shares of Other Corporations: Whenever the Corporation is the holder of shares of any other Corporation, any right or power of the Corporation as such shareholder (including the attendance, acting and voting at shareholders' meetings and execution of waivers, consents, proxies or other instruments) may be exercised on behalf of the Corporation by the President, any Vice President, or such other person as the Board may authorize.

ARTICLE V—COMMITTEES

The Board of Directors may, by resolution, designate an Executive Committee and one or more other committees. Such committees shall have such functions and may exercise such power of the Board of Directors as can be lawfully delegated, and to the extent provided in the resolution or resolutions creating such committee or committees. Meetings of committees may be held without notice at such time and at such place as shall from time to time be determined by the committees. The committees of the corporation shall keep regular minutes of their proceedings, and report these minutes to the Board of Directors when required.

ARTICLE VI—BOOKS, RECORDS, AND REPORTS

Section 1—Annual Report: The Corporation shall send an annual report to the Members of the Corporation not later than _____ months after the close of each fiscal year of the Corporation. Such report shall include a balance sheet as of the close of the fiscal year of the Corporation and a revenue and disbursement statement for the year ending on such closing date. Such financial statements shall be prepared from and in accordance with the books of the Corporation, and in conformity with generally accepted accounting principles applied on a consistent basis.

Section 2—Permanent Records: The corporation shall keep current and correct records of the accounts, minutes of the meetings and proceedings and membership records of the corporation. Such records shall be kept at the registered office or the principal place of business of the corporation. Any such records shall be in written form or in a form capable of being converted into written form.

Section 3—Inspection of Corporate Records: Any person who is a Voting Member of the Corporation shall have the right at any reasonable time, and on written demand stating the purpose thereof, to examine and make copies from the relevant books and records of accounts, minutes, and records of the Corporation. Upon the written request of any Voting Member, the Corporation shall mail to such Member a copy of the most recent balance sheet and revenue and disbursement statement.

ARTICLE VII—SHARES OF STOCK

Section 1—Certificates: Each shareholder of the corporation shall be entitled to have a certificate representing all shares which he or she owns. The form of such certificate shall be adopted by a majority vote of the Board of Directors and shall be signed by the President and Secretary of the Corporation and sealed with the seal of the corporation. No certificate representing shares shall be issued until the full amount of consideration therefore has been paid.

Section 2—Stock Ledger: The corporation shall maintain a ledger of the stock records of the Corporation. Transfers of shares of the Corporation shall be made on the stock ledger of the Corporation only at the direction of the holder of record upon surrender of the outstanding certificate(s). The Corporation shall be entitled to treat the holder of record of any share or shares as the absolute owner thereof for all purposes and, accordingly, shall not be bound to recognize any legal, equitable or other claim to, or interest in, such share or shares on the part of any other person, whether or not it shall have express or other notice thereof, except as otherwise expressly provided by law.

ARTICLE VIII—DIVIDENDS

Upon approval by the Board of Directors the corporation may pay dividends on its shares in the form of cash, property or additional shares at any time that the corporation is solvent and if such dividends would not render the corporation insolvent.

ARTICLE IX—FISCAL YEAR

The fiscal year of the Corporation shall be the period selected by the Board of Directors as the tax year of the Corporation for federal income tax purposes.

ARTICLE X—CORPORATE SEAL

The Board of Directors may adopt, use and modify a corporate seal. Failure to affix the seal to corporate documents shall not affect the validity of such document.

ARTICLE XI—AMENDMENTS

The Articles of Incorporation may be amended by the Shareholders as provided by _____ statutes. These Bylaws may be altered, amended, or replaced by the Board of Directors; provided, however, that any Bylaws or amendments thereto as adopted by the Board of Directors may be altered, amended, or repealed by vote of the Shareholders. Bylaws adopted by the Members may not be amended or repealed by the Board.

ARTICLE XII—INDEMNIFICATION

Any officer, director or employee of the Corporation shall be indemnified to the full extent allowed by the laws of the State of _____.

Certified to be the Bylaws of the corporation adopted by the Board of Directors on _____, 20____.

_____
Secretary

State Tax Forms

In most states, there is a state corporate income tax. In some states, you will be exempt from corporate income tax if you are an S corporation, but you will need to file a form to let the government know that you are exempt.

If you will be selling or renting goods or services at retail, you may be required to collect state *sales and use* taxes. To do this, you will need to register, and in most cases, pay a registration fee. In some states and in some businesses, you will be required to post a bond covering the taxes you will be collecting. There may be other taxes that your state requires. Contact your state taxing authority and ask for the forms available for new corporations.

Corporate Supplies

A corporation needs to keep a permanent record of its legal affairs. This includes: the original articles of incorporation; minutes of all meetings; records of the stock issued, transferred, and cancelled; fictitious names registered; and, any other legal matters. The records are usually kept in a ring binder. Any ring binder will do, but it is possible to purchase a specially prepared *corporate kit*, which has the name of the corporation printed on it and usually contains some forms, such as minutes and stock certificates. Most of these items are included with this book, so purchasing such a kit is unnecessary unless you want to have a fancy leather binder or specially printed stock certificates. Figure 10.5 lists some suppliers of corporate kits.

Corporate Seal

A *corporate seal* must be specially made for each corporation. Most corporations use a metal seal like a notary's seal to emboss the paper. This can be ordered from an office supply company. Some states now allow rubber stamps for corporate seals. These are cheaper, lighter, and easier to read. Rubber stamp seals can also be ordered from office supply stores, printers, and specialized rubber stamp companies. The corporate seal should contain the full, exact name of the corporation, the word "SEAL," and the year of incorporation. It may be round or rectangular.

Figure 10.5: Corporate Kits

Some sources for corporate kits include the following.

Blumberg Excelsior
4435 Old Winter Garden Road
Orlando, FL 32811
407-299-8220
800-327-9220
Fax: 407-291-6912
www.blumberg.com/index2.html

Corpex
1440 Fifth Avenue
Bay Shore, NY 11706
800-221-8181
Fax: 800-826-7739
Email: Corpex@CorpexNet.com
www.corpexnet.com

CorpKit Legal Supplies
46 Taft Avenue
Islip, NY 11751
888-888-9120
Fax: 888-777-4617
Email: info@corpkit.com
www.corpkit.com

Stock Certificates and Offers to Purchase Stock

In some states, corporations are no longer required to issue stock certificates to represent shares of ownership. However, as a practical matter, it is a good idea to do so. This shows some formality and gives each person tangible evidence of ownership. If you do issue shares, the face of each certificate must show the corporate name; the state law under which the corporation is organized; the name of the shareholder(s); and, the number, class, and series of the stock. The certificate must be signed by one or more officers designated by the bylaws or the board of directors.

If there are two or more classes or series of stock, the front or back of the certificate must disclose that, "upon request and without charge, the corporation will provide to the shareholder the preferences, limitations, and relative rights of each class or series, the preferences of any preferred stock, and the board of director's authority to determine rights for any subsequent classes or series." If there are any restrictions, they must be stated on the certificate, or a statement must be included that a copy of the restrictions is available without charge.

The stock certificates can be fancy and intricately engraved with eagles and scrolls, or they can be typed or even handwritten. If you purchase a corporate kit, you will receive certificates printed with your company's name on them. Figure 10.6 shows a blank sample of the front and back of a stock certificate.

Before any stock is issued, the purchaser should submit an Offer to Purchase Stock. The Offer to Purchase Stock states that the offer is made pursuant to Section 1244 of the Internal Revenue Code. The advantage of this section is that in the event the business fails or the value of the stock drops, the shareholder can write off up to $50,000 ($100,000 for married couples) as ordinary income, rather than as a long-term capital loss, which would be limited to $3,000 a year.

Some thought should be given to the way in which the ownership of the stock will be held. Stock owned in one person's name alone is subject to probate upon death. Making two people joint owners of the stock (joint tenants with full rights of survivorship) would avoid probate upon the death of one of them. However, taking a joint owner's name off in the event of a disagreement (such as divorce) could be troublesome. If a couple jointly operates a business, joint ownership is best. However, if one person is the sole party involved in the business, the desire to avoid probate should be weighed against the risk of losing half the business in a divorce.

Most states allow securities to be registered in *pay on death* or *transfer on death* form, similar to bank accounts. This means the stock can be owned by one person, but designated to pass to another person at death without that person getting any current rights in the stock. Check with your stock broker or attorney, or in your state statutes. The law is called the *Uniform TOD Securities Registration Act*. All states have passed this law with the exception of Louisiana and Texas.

Figure 10.6: **Stock Certificate**

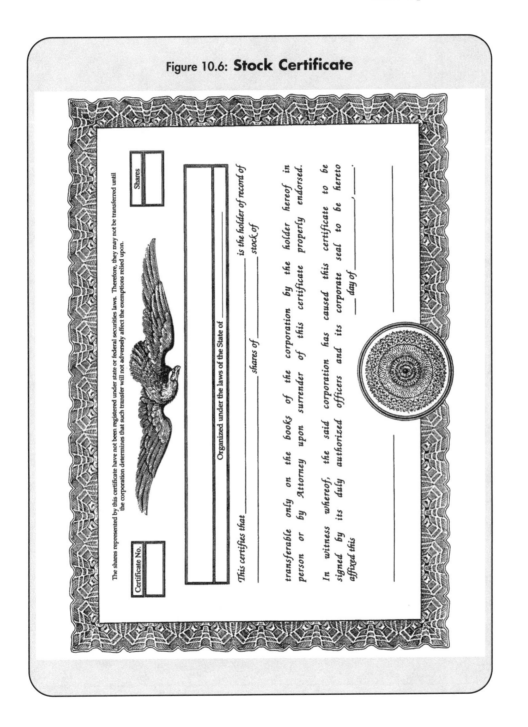

For value received,_____ hereby sell, assign and transfer unto _____ shares represented by

this certificate and do hereby irrevocably constitute and appoint _____

attorney to transfer the said shares on the books of the corporation with full power of substitution in the premises.

Dated _____

Witness:
_____

Taxes Some states levy a tax on the issue or transfer of stock. The amount and means of calculating the tax vary from state to state. Check with the secretary of state or your county government tax office to find out if any such tax is charged, how to calculate the amount of tax, and how to go about paying it.

This is a tax you can easily lower, but do not avoid paying it. If you do, someone may use this to pierce the corporate veil and hold you liable for debts of the corporation. You can keep the tax low by structuring your corporate stock to the minimum tax. In some states, this means fewer shares, and in other states it means lower par value.

> **EXAMPLE:** In Ohio, the tax is on the number of shares. To keep the tax low, you would issue a small number of shares and pay a higher amount for each share. In Florida, the tax is based on the payment for the shares, so you could issue a large number of shares with a low par value. If you wanted to contribute more capital to the corporation, you should designate it as paid-in surplus rather than as payment for more shares.
>
> The Ohio tax is $10 per share for the first thousand shares, with a minimum tax of $85. This means you can have 850 shares without paying extra tax. A person forming an Ohio corporation with $5,000 in capital could authorize 850 shares at $2 par value, issue five hundred, and pay $10 per share.
>
> Florida does not have a tax on authorized shares, but has a documentary stamp tax on issued shares. Thus you could authorize one million shares at $0.001 par value and pay $1,000 for all million shares. Additional capital could be contributed as paid-in surplus or as a loan to the corporation.

Organizational Meeting

The real birth of the corporation takes place at the initial meeting of the incorporators and the initial board of directors. At this meeting, the stock is issued and the officers and board of directors are elected. Other business may also take place, such as opting for S corporation status or adopting employee benefit plans.

Usually, forms for minutes, stock certificates, taxes, and so on are prepared before the organizational meeting and used as a script for the meeting. They are then signed at the end of the meeting. Figure 10.7 provides an agenda for a typical initial meeting.

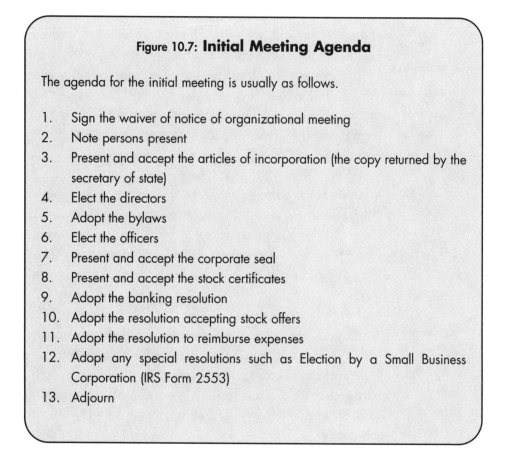

Figure 10.7: **Initial Meeting Agenda**

The agenda for the initial meeting is usually as follows.

1. Sign the waiver of notice of organizational meeting
2. Note persons present
3. Present and accept the articles of incorporation (the copy returned by the secretary of state)
4. Elect the directors
5. Adopt the bylaws
6. Elect the officers
7. Present and accept the corporate seal
8. Present and accept the stock certificates
9. Adopt the banking resolution
10. Adopt the resolution accepting stock offers
11. Adopt the resolution to reimburse expenses
12. Adopt any special resolutions such as Election by a Small Business Corporation (IRS Form 2553)
13. Adjourn

The stock certificates are usually issued at the end of the meeting, but in some cases, such as when a prospective shareholder does not yet have money to pay for them, they are issued when paid for.

To issue the stock, the certificates should be completed by adding the name of the corporation, the state of incorporation, the number of shares the certificate represents, and the person to whom the certificate is issued. Each certificate should be numbered in order to keep track of it.

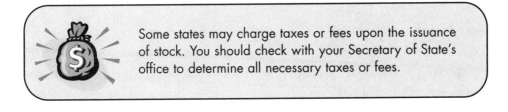

Some states may charge taxes or fees upon the issuance of stock. You should check with your Secretary of State's office to determine all necessary taxes or fees.

Minute Book

After the organizational meeting, you should set up your minute book. As noted previously, this can be a fancy leather book or a simple ring binder. The minute book usually contains the following.

1. Title page ("Corporate Records of _____")
2. Table of contents
3. The letter from the secretary of state acknowledging receipt and filing of the articles of incorporation
4. Copy of the articles of incorporation
5. Copy of any fictitious name registration
6. Copy of any trademark registration
7. Waiver of notice of organizational meeting
8. Minutes of organizational meeting
9. Bylaws
10. Sample stock certificate
11. Offer to purchase stock
12. Tax forms:
    a.   IRS Form SS-4 identifying the issued Employer Identification Number
    b.   IRS Form 2553 and acceptance notification from the IRS
    c.   Any state form necessary, along with state tax number

13. Stock transfer ledger

14. Stock certificate stubs

Bank Account

A corporation will need a bank account. Typically, checks payable to a corporation cannot be cashed by a shareholder. Instead, they must be deposited into an account.

Bank Fees

Unfortunately, many banks charge ridiculous rates to corporations for the right to put their money in the bank. You can tell how much extra a corporation is being charged when you compare a corporate account with a personal account with similar activity.

Fortunately, some banks have set up reasonable fees for small corporations. Some charge no fees if a balance of $1,000 or $2,500 is maintained. Because the fees can easily amount to hundreds of dollars a year, it pays to shop around. Even if the bank is relatively far from the business, using bank-by-mail and online banking can make the distance meaningless.

Another way to save money in bank charges is to order checks from a private source rather than through the bank. These are usually much cheaper than the checks the bank offers, because most banks get a commission on check orders. If the bank officer does not like the idea when you are opening the account, just wait until your first batch of bank checks runs out and switch over at that time.

Paperwork

All you should need to open a corporate bank account is a copy of your articles of incorporation and your federal tax identification number (and perhaps a business license). If other documentation is needed, such as a banking resolution, the bank will usually provide you its preferred form for completion.

Licenses

In some states, counties and municipalities are authorized to levy a license fee or tax on the privilege of doing business. Before opening your business, you need to find out if any such license is required. Businesses that perform work in several cities, such as builders, may need to obtain a license from each city or county in which they perform work or have an office.

Every state also has laws requiring the licensing of certain types of businesses or professions. Some states regulate more types than others. Just because you did not need a license in one state is not a guarantee that you will not need one if you move to a new state.

Be sure to find out if zoning allows your type of business before buying or leasing property. Usually, the licensing departments will check the zoning before issuing your license.

Figure 10.8: **Checklist for Forming a Simple Corporation**

- ☐ Decide on corporate name.
- ☐ Prepare and file articles of incorporation.
- ☐ Complete and file Application for Employer Identification Number (IRS Form SS-4).
- ☐ Prepare shareholder agreement, if necessary.
- ☐ Meet with accountant to discuss capitalization and tax planning.
- ☐ If necessary, meet with securities lawyer regarding stock sales.
- ☐ Obtain corporate seal and ring binder for minutes.
- ☐ Pay any applicable taxes for sale or issuance of stock.
- ☐ Hold organizational meeting.
- ☐ Complete bylaws, waivers, minutes, and offers to purchase stock.
- ☐ Sign all documents and place in minute book.
- ☐ Issue stock certificates.
- ☐ Complete bill of sale if property is traded for stock.
- ☐ File fictitious name if one will be used.
- ☐ Get licenses.
- ☐ Open bank account.
- ☐ For S corporation status, file IRS Form 2553 within seventy-five days of formation.

Chapter

Shareholder Interest in a Corporation

While many people are eager to put money into a startup business and the businesses are even more eager to get it, there is a labyrinth of laws controlling exactly how and from whom you can accept funds. Numerous stock frauds over the years have resulted in harsh criminal penalties for those who do not follow the laws.

Securities Laws

The issuance of securities is subject to both federal and state securities laws. A *security* is stock in the company (common and preferred) and debt (notes, bonds, etc.). The laws covering securities are so broad that any instrument that represents an investment in an enterprise in which the investor is relying on the efforts of others for profit is considered a security. Even a promissory note has been held to be a security. Once an investment is determined to involve a security, strict rules apply. There can be criminal penalties and civil damages can be awarded to purchasers if the rules are not followed.

The rules are designed to protect people who put up money as an investment in a business. In the stock market crash in 1929, many people lost their life savings in swindles, and the government wants to be sure that it will not happen again. Unfortunately, the laws can also make it difficult to raise capital for many honest businesses.

QUICK Tip

The law is complicated and strict compliance is required. You most likely would not be able to get through the registration process on your own. You may wish to consider some alternatives when attempting to raise capital without an attorney.

One alternative way to raise money is to borrow the money as a personal loan from friends or relatives. The disadvantage is that you will have to pay them back personally if the business fails. However, you may have to do that anyway if they are close relatives or if you do not follow the securities laws.

You could also tailor your stock issuance to fall within the exemptions in the securities laws. There are some exemptions in the securities laws for small businesses that may apply to your transaction. (The anti-fraud provisions always apply, even if the transaction is exempt from registration.) Some exemptions are explained in the following section, but you should make at least one appointment with a securities lawyer to be sure you have covered everything and that there have not been any changes in the law. You can often pay $100 or $200 for an hour or so of a securities attorney's time and just ask questions about your plans. He or she can tell you what not to do and what your options are. Then you can make an informed decision.

The goal of the laws covering sales of securities is that investors be given full disclosure of the risks involved in an investment. To accomplish this, the law usually requires that the securities must either be registered with the federal *Securities and Exchange Commission* (SEC) or a similar state regulatory body, and that lengthy disclosure statements be compiled and distributed.

Federal Exemptions from Securities Laws

In most situations involving one person, a husband and wife, or a few partners running a business, where all parties are active in the enterprise, securities laws do not apply to the issuance of stock to themselves. These are the simple corporations that are the subject of this book. As a practical matter, if your father or aunt wants to put up some money for some stock in your business, you probably will not get in trouble. They probably will not seek triple damages and criminal penalties if your business fails.

However, you may wish to obtain money from additional investors to enable your business to grow. This can be done in many circumstances, as long as you follow the rules carefully. In some cases, you do not have to file anything with the SEC, but in others, you must file a notice.

Federal Private Offering Exemption

If you sell your stock to a small group of people without any advertising, you fall into the *private offering exemption*. Some of the requirements for this exemption include the following.

- All persons to whom offers are made must be financially astute, participants in the business, or have a substantial net worth.
- No advertising or general solicitation is used to promote the stock.
- The number of persons to whom the offers are made is limited.
- The shares are purchased for investment and not for immediate resale.
- The persons to whom the stock is offered are given all relevant information (including financial information) regarding the issuance and the corporation.
- A filing claiming the exemption is made upon the United States Securities and Exchange Commission.

Again, there are numerous court cases explaining each aspect of these rules, including such questions as what is a *financially astute* person.

Federal Intrastate Offering Exemption

If you only offer your securities to residents of one state, you may be exempt from federal securities laws. Federal laws usually only apply to interstate commerce. Intrastate offerings are covered by SEC Rule 147, and if it is followed carefully, your sale will be exempt from federal registration.

Federal Small Offerings Exemptions

In recent years, the Securities and Exchange Commission has liberalized the rules in order to make it easier for business to grow. The SEC has adopted Regulation D, which states that there are three types of exemptions, found in SEC Rules 504, 505, and 506.

SEC Rule 504 Offerings of securities of up to $1,000,000 in a twelve-month period can be exempt under SEC Rule 504. Offers can be made to any number of persons, no specific information must be provided, and investors do not have to be sophisticated.

SEC Rule 505 Under SEC Rule 505, offerings of up to $5,000,000 can be made in a twelve-month period, but no public advertising may be used and only thirty-five non-accredited investors may purchase stock. Any number of *accredited investors* may purchase stock. Accredited investors are sophisticated individuals with high net worth or high income, large trusts or investment companies, or persons involved in the business.

SEC Rule 506 SEC Rule 506 has no limit on the amount of money that may be raised, but like Rule 505, does not allow advertising and limits non-accredited investors to thirty-five.

State Securities Laws

One reason there are exemptions from federal securities laws is because there are so many state laws covering securities that additional registration is not needed. Every state has securities laws, which are called *blue sky laws*. If you wish to offer your stock in all fifty states, you must be registered in all fifty states, unless you can fit into one of the exemptions. However, exemptions are very limited.

Figure 11.1: **State Securities Registration Offices**

The following are the addresses of the state offices that handle registration of securities. You can contact them for information on their requirements.

Alabama Securities Commission
770 Washington Street
Suite 570
Montgomery, AL 36130
Phone: 334-242-2984 or 800-222-1253
Fax: 334-242-0240 or 334-353-4690
www.asc.state.al.us

Alaska Department of Commerce and Economic Development Division of Banking, Securities, and Corporations
P.O. Box 110807
Juneau, AK 99811
Phone: 907-465-2521
Fax: 907-465-2549
www.dced.state.ak.us/bsc

Arizona Corporation Commission Securities Division
1300 West Washington Street
3rd Floor
Phoenix, AZ 85007
Phone: 602-542-4242
Fax: 602-594-7470
www.ccsd.cc.state.az.us

Arkansas Securities Department
Heritage West Building
201 East Markham
3rd Floor
Little Rock, AR 72201
Phone: 501-324-9260
Fax: 501-324-9268

California Department of Corporations Securities Regulation Division
320 West 4th Street
Suite 750
Los Angeles, CA 90013
Phone: 213-576-7500
Fax: 213-576-7179
www.corp.ca.gov/srd/security.htm

Colorado Division of Securities
1580 Lincoln Street
Suite 420
Denver, CO 80203
Phone: 303-894-2320
Fax: 303-861-2126
www.dora.state.co.us/securities

Connecticut Securities Division
260 Constitution Plaza
Hartford, CT 06103
Phone: 860-240-8230
Fax: 860-240-8295
www.state.ct.us/dob

Delaware Department of Justice Division of Securities
820 North French Street, 5th Floor
Wilmington, DE 19801
Phone: 302-577-8242
Fax: 302-577-6987
www.state.de.us/securities/index.htm

District of Columbia Department of Insurance and Securities Regulation
810 First Street
Suite 701
Washington, DC 20002
Phone: 202-727-8000
Fax: 202-535-1196
http://disb.dc.gov/disr/site/default.asp

Florida Division of Securities and Finance
200 East Gaines Street
Tallahassee, FL 32399
Phone: 850-410-9805
Fax: 850-410-9748
www.dbf.state.fl.us/licensing

Georgia Secretary of State Securities and Business Regulation Division
2 Martin Luther King Jr. Drive, S.E.
Suite 802, West Tower
Atlanta, GA 30334
Phone: 404-656-3920
Fax: 404-657-8410
www.sos.state.ga.us/securities
or www.georgiasecurities.org

Hawaii Department of Commerce and Consumer Affairs Commissioner of Securities
P. O. Box 40
Honolulu, HI 96810
Phone: 808-586-2744
Fax: 808-586-3977
www.hawaii.gov/dcca/areas/sec

Idaho Department of Finance
700 West State Street
2nd Floor
P.O. Box 83702
Boise, ID 83720
Phone: 208-332-8000
Fax: 208-332-8099
http://finance.state.id.us

Illinois Securities Department
Jefferson Terrace
Suite 300 A
300 West Jefferson Street
Springfield, IL 62702
Phone: 217-782-2256
Fax: 217-782-8876
www.sos.state.il.us/departments/
   securities/home.html

Indiana Securities Division
302 West Washington Street
Room E-111
Indianapolis, IN 46204
Phone: 317-232-6681 or 800-223-8791
Fax: 317-233-3675
www.IN.gov/sos/securities

Iowa Securities Bureau
340 Maple Street
Des Moines, IA 50319-0066
Phone: 515-281-4441
Fax: 515-281-3059
www.iowa.gov

Kansas Securities Commissioner Office of the Securities Commissioner
618 South Kansas Avenue
Topeka, KS 66603
Phone: 785-296-3307
Fax: 785-296-6872
www.securities.state.ks.us

Kentucky Department of Financial Institutions
1025 Capital Center Drive
Suite 200
Frankfort, KY 40601
Phone: 502-573-3390 or 800-223-2579
Fax: 502-573-8787
www.dfi.state.ky.us

Louisiana Office of Financial Institutions
Securities Division
Commissioner of Securities
8660 United Plaza Boulevard
2nd Floor
Baton Rouge, LA 70809
Phone: 225-925-4660
Fax: 225-925-4548
www.ofi.state.la.us

Maine Department of Professional and Financial Regulation
Office of Securities
121 State House Station
Augusta, ME 04333
Phone: 207-624-8551
Fax: 207-624-8590
www.state.me.us/pfr/sec/sec_index.htm

Maryland Securities Division
200 Saint Paul Place
Baltimore, MD 21202
Phone: 410-576-6360
www.oag.state.md.us/securities/
  index.htm

Massachusetts Securities Division
One Ashburton Place
17th Floor
Boston, MA 02108
Phone: 617-727-3548 or 800-269-5428
Fax: 617-248-0177
www.state.ma.us/sec/sct/sctidx.htm

Michigan Department of Consumer and Industry Services
Offices of Financial and Insurance Services
P.O. Box 30220
Lansing, MI 48909
Phone: 517-373-0220 or 877-999-6442
Fax: 517-335-4978
www.michigan.gov/cis

Minnesota Department of Commerce
85 7th Place East
Suite 500
St. Paul, MN 55101
Phone: 651-296-4973
www.state.mn.us

Mississippi Securities Division
P.O. Box 136
Jackson, MS 39205
Phone: 800-804-6364
Fax: 601-359-2663
www.sos.state.ms.us

Office of the Missouri Secretary of State
Securities Division
600 West Main Street
2nd Floor
Jefferson City, MO 65101
Phone: 573-751-4136
Fax: 573-526-3124
www.sos.mo.gov/securities

Montana Office of the State Auditor
Securities Division
840 Helena Avenue
Helena, MT 59601
Phone: 406-444-3246
Fax: 406-444-3497
www.discoveringmontana.com/sao/
  securities

Nebraska Bureau of Securities Commerce Court
1230 "O" Street
Suite 400
P.O. Box 95006
Lincoln, NE 68509
Phone: 402-471-3445
www.ndbf.org

Nevada Securities Division
555 East Washington Avenue
Suite 5200
Las Vegas, NV 89101
Phone: 702-486-2440
Fax: 702-486-2452
www.sos.state.nv.us/securities/index.htm

New Hampshire Bureau of Securities Regulation
State House
Room 204
Concord, NH 03301
Phone: 603-271-1463
Fax: 603-271-7933
webster.state.nh.us/sos/securities

New Jersey Bureau of Securities
P.O. Box 47029
Newark, NJ 07101
Phone: 973-504-3600
Fax: 973-504-3601
www.state.nj.us/lps/ca/bos.htm

New Mexico Securities Division Regulation and Licensing Department
2550 Cerrillos Road
3rd Floor
Santa Fe, NM 87505
Phone: 505-827-7010
Fax: 505-827-7095
www.rld.state.nm.us/sec/index.htm

New York State Attorney General's Office
Investors and Securities
The Capital
Albany, NY 12224
Phone: 212-416-8000
Fax: 212-416-8816
www.oag.state.ny.us/investors/investors.html

North Carolina Securities Division Department of the Secretary of State
P.O. Box 29622
Raleigh, NC 27626
Phone: 919-733-3924
Fax: 919-733-5172
www.secretary.state.nc.us/sec

North Dakota Securities Commission
State Capitol
5th Floor
600 East Boulevard Avenue
Bismarck, ND 58505
Phone: 701-328-2910
Fax: 701-328-2946
www.ndsecurities.com

Ohio Department of Commerce Division of Securities
77 South High Street
22nd Floor
Columbus, OH 43215
Phone: 614-644-7381
www.securities.state.oh.us

Oklahoma Department of Securities
Suite 860, First National Center
120 North Robinson
Oklahoma City, OK 73102
Phone: 405-280-7700
Fax: 405-280-7742
www.securities.state.ok.us

Oregon Department of Consumer and Business Services
Division of Finance and Corporate Securities
P.O. Box 14480
Salem, OR 97309
Phone: 503-378-4140
Fax: 503-947-7862
www.cbs.state.or.us/external/dfcs

Pennsylvania Division of Corporation Finance
Pennsylvania Securities Commission
Eastgate Office Building
2nd Floor
1010 North 7th Street
Harrisburg, PA 17102
Phone: 717-787-8061
Fax: 717-783-5122
www.psc.state.pa.us

Puerto Rico Commissioner of Financial Institutions
Centro Europa Building
1492 Ponce de Leon Avenue
Suite 600
San Juan, PR 00907
Phone: 787-723-3131
Fax: 787-723-4255
www.cif.gov.pr/valores_eng.html

South Carolina Securities Division
P.O. Box 11549
Columbia, SC 29211
Phone: 803-734-9916
Fax: 803-734-3677
www.scsecurities.org/index.html

South Dakota Division of Securities
445 East Capitol Avenue
Pierre, SD 57501
Phone: 605-773-4823
Fax: 605-773-5953
www.state.sd.us/dcr/securities/
    security.htm

Tennessee Department of Commerce and Insurance Securities Division
500 James Robertson Parkway
Suite 680
Davy Crockett Tower
Nashville, TN 37243
Phone: 615-741-3187
Fax: 615-532-8375
www.state.tn.us/commerce

Texas State Securities Board
P.O. Box 13167
Austin, TX 78711
Phone: 512-305-8300
Fax: 512-305-8310
www.ssb.state.tx.us

Utah Department of Commerce Division of Securities
Box 146760
Salt Lake City, UT 84114
Phone: 801-530-6600
Fax: 801-530-6980
www.securities.state.ut.us

Vermont Securities Division
Department of Banking, Insurance,
Securities and Health Care
Administration
89 Main Street
Drawer 20
Montpelier, VT 05620
Phone: 802-828-3420
www.bishca.state.vt.us/securitiesdiv/
   securindex.htm

Virginia State Corporation
Commission
P.O. Box 1197
Richmond, VA 23218
Phone: 804-371-9967
Fax: 804-371-9911
www.scc.virginia.gov

Washington Department of
Financial Institutions
Securities Division
P.O. Box 9033
Olympia, WA 98507
Phone: 360-902-8760
Fax: 360-902-0524
www.dfi.wa.gov

West Virginia Securities Division
State Capitol Building 1
Room W-100
Charleston, WV 25305
Phone: 304-558-2257
Fax: 304-558-4211
www.wvauditor.com

Wisconsin Division of Securities
P.O. Box 8041
Madison, WI 53708
Phone: 608-264-7969
Fax: 608-264-7968
www.wdfi.org/fi/securities

Wyoming Securities Division
Secretary of the State
The Capital Building
Room 109
200 West 24th Street
Cheyenne, WY 82002
Phone: 307-777-7370
Fax: 307-777-5339
http://soswy.state.wy.us/securiti/
   securiti.htm

Private Placement Exemption

The most common state exemption is the *private placement exemption*. This can apply if all of the following are true:

- there are thirty-five or fewer purchasers of shares;
- no commissions are paid to anyone to promote the stock;
- no advertising or general solicitation is used to promote the stock;
- all material information (including financial information) regarding the stock issuance and the company is given to or accessible to all shareholders; and,
- a three-day right of recision is given.

These rules may sound simple on the surface, but there are many rules, regulations, and court cases explaining each one in more detail. For example, what does thirty-five purchasers mean? It sounds simple, but it can mean more than thirty-five persons. Spouses, persons whose net worth exceeds a million dollars, and founders of the corporation may not be counted in some circumstances. Each state has its own blue sky requirements and exemptions. If you are going to raise money from investors, check with a qualified securities lawyer.

As you can see, the exemption does not give you much latitude in raising money. Therefore, you will have to register with the SEC. To find out more about the registration process in each state, contact the office in each state in which you intend to sell stock.

Internet Stock Sales

With the advent of the Internet, promoters of stock have a new way of reaching large numbers of people financially able to afford investments in securities. However, all securities laws apply to the Internet, and they are being enforced. Recently, state attorneys general have issued *cease and desist orders* to promoters not registered in their states.

Under current law, you must be registered in a state in order to sell stock to its residents. If you are not registered in a state, you must turn down any residents from that state who want to buy your stock.

Payment for Shares

When issuing stock, it is important that full payment be made by the purchasers. If the shares have a par value and the payment is in cash, then the cash must not be less than the par value. In most states, promissory notes cannot be used in payment for shares. The shares must not be issued until the payment has been received by the corporation.

Trading Property for Shares

In many cases, organizers of a corporation have property they want to contribute for use in starting up the business. This is often the case when an ongoing business is incorporated. To avoid future problems, the property should be traded at a fair value for the shares. The directors should pass a resolution stating that they agree with the value of the property. When the stock certificate is issued in exchange for the property, a bill of sale should be executed by the owner of the property, detailing everything that is being exchanged for the stock.

Taxable Transactions

In cases where property is exchanged for something of value, such as stock, there is often income tax due, as if there had been a sale of the property. Fortunately, the federal tax code allows tax-free exchange of property for stock if the persons receiving the stock for the property or for cash end up owning at least 80% of the voting and other stock in the corporation (Internal Revenue Service Code, Section 351). If more than 20% of the stock is issued in exchange for services instead of property and cash, then the transfers of property will be taxable and treated as a sale for cash.

Trading Services for Shares

In some cases, the founders of a corporation may wish to issue stock to one or more persons in exchange for their services to the corporation. It has always been possible to issue shares for services that have previously been performed. Some states make it unlawful to issue shares for promises to perform services in the future. Check your state's statutes regarding this.

Chapter  12

Running a Corporation

One of the rules for running a corporation is that you should follow the formalities of the corporation if you wish to be treated as a corporation. You should follow these formalities on a daily basis and not just create the paperwork if you are sued.

Day-to-Day Activities

There are not many differences between running a corporation and any other type of business. The most important point to remember is to keep the corporation's affairs separate from your personal affairs. The corporation should not make frequent loans to its shareholders, and funds of the corporation and individual shareholders should not be commingled. Funds taken out or put into the corporation should be documented. The decision of whether these should be salary, loans, dividends, or otherwise, should be made with the help of an accountant or good tax guide based upon your financial situation.

QUICK Tip

Always use the complete corporate name, including designations such as Inc. or Corp., on *everything*. *Always* sign corporate documents with your corporate title.

Another important point to remember is to always refer to the corporation as a corporation. *Always* use the complete corporate name, including designations such as Inc. or Corp., on *everything*. *Always* sign corporate documents with your corporate title. If you do not, you may lose your protection from liability. There have been many cases in which a person forgot to put the word *pres.* or *president* after his or her name when entering into contracts for the corporation. As a result, the person was determined to be personally liable for performance of the contract.

Corporate Records

A corporation must keep minutes of the proceedings of its shareholders, board of directors, and committees of directors. The minutes should be in writing. Some states allow minutes to be kept in forms other than writing, provided they can be converted into written form within a reasonable time. This would mean that they could be kept in a computer or possibly on a videotape. However, it is always best to keep a duplicate copy or at least one written copy. Accidents can easily erase magnetic media.

Record of Shareholders

The corporation must also keep a record of its shareholders, including their names and addresses, and the number, class, and series of shares owned.

This can be kept at the registered office, principal place of business, or office of its stock transfer agent (if any).

Examination of Records

Any shareholder of a corporation has the right to examine and copy the corporation's books and records, after giving proper notice before the date on which he or she wishes to inspect and copy. The shareholder must have a *good faith* reason to inspect. He or she must describe his or her purpose, the records he or she wishes to inspect, and how the purpose is related to the records.

The shareholder may have his or her attorney or agent examine the records, and may receive photocopies of the records. The corporation may charge a reasonable fee for making photocopies. If the records are not in written form, the corporation must convert them to written form. Customarily, the corporation must bear the cost of converting all of the following to written form:

- the articles of incorporation and any amendments;
- the bylaws and any amendments;
- resolutions by the board of directors creating different rights in the stock;
- minutes of all shareholders' meetings;
- records of any action taken by the shareholders without a meeting for the past three years;
- written communications to all shareholders;
- names and addresses of all officers and directors; and,
- the most recent report filed with the state corporate office.

The shareholder may be required to pay for converting any other records to writing.

If the corporation refuses to allow a shareholder to examine the records, most states allow the shareholder to seek an order from the appropriate state court. In such a case, the corporation would normally have to pay the shareholder's costs and attorney's fees.

Balance Sheets

Most states require a corporation to furnish its shareholders with financial statements. This includes an end-of-the-year balance sheet and yearly income and cash flow statements, unless exempted by shareholder resolution.

Annual Meetings

Each year, the corporation must hold annual meetings of the shareholders and directors. These meetings may be formal and held in the office, or they may be informal and held in a restaurant. A sole officer and director can hold them in his or her mind without verbally reciting all of the motions or taking a formal vote. The important thing is that the meetings are held and that minutes are kept, even by a one-person corporation.

QUICK Tip

Regular minutes and meetings are evidence that the corporation is legitimate if the issue ever comes up in court.

Annual Report

Most states require that every corporation file an *annual report* each year. Many states make this a biannual requirement. Fortunately, this is a simple, often one-page form that is sent to the corporation by the secretary of state, and may merely need to be signed. It contains such information as the federal tax identification number, officers' and directors' names and addresses, the registered agent's name, and the address of the registered office. It must be signed and returned with the required fee by the date specified by the state. If this is not done, then the corporation is dissolved after notice is given. Many states allow some corporate information (such as the registered office and agent) to be changed at this time without additional fees to the corporation. The corporation should be aware of this fact in order to avoid incurring needless expenses.

Glossary

The following definitions explain how the words are used in this book. (They may have other meanings in other contexts.)

A

accredited investor. Sophisticated individuals with high net worth or high income, large trusts or investment companies, or persons involved in the business.

addendum. A document attached to another document to add some new terms.

annual report. A document filed by a corporation each year, usually listing the officers, directors, and registered agent.

articles of incorporation. The document that demonstrates the organization of a corporation, called certificate of incorporation or charter in some states.

articles of organization. The legal document used to form a limited liability company that sets out basic information about it, such as its name.

assignment. The transfer of legal rights to another person or entity.

B

blue sky laws. Laws governing the sales of securities.

board of directors. Governing body of a corporation that establishes corporate policies, appoints executive officers, and makes major financial decisions.

bylaws. Rules governing the conduct of affairs of a corporation.

C

C corporation. A corporation that pays taxes on its profits.

capital. Initial funding of the business.

charging order. A court order directed at an interest in an LLC.

common stock. The basic ownership shares of a corporation.

contract. An agreement between two or more parties.

corporation. An artificial legal person that is set up to conduct a business owned by shareholders and run by officers and directors.

D

dissolution. The closing of a limited liability company.

distributions. Money paid out to owners of a corporation or limited liability company.

domestic corporation. A corporation incorporated in the state in which business is done.

E

employee. Person who works for another under that person's control and direction.

employer identification number. Number issued by the Internal Revenue Service to identify taxpayers who do not have Social Security numbers.

estate planning. Preparing documents such as a will, trust, and other arrangements to control the passing of one's property at death.

exemption. The ability to sell certain limited types of securities without full compliance with securities registration laws.

F

fictitious name. A name used by a business that is not its personal or legal name.

foreign corporation. Incorporated in a state other than where business is done.

G

general partnership. A business that is owned by two or more persons.

I

independent contractor. A person who does work as a separate business rather than as an employee.

industry code. A number assigned to each type of business.

insolvent. Being without enough assets of income to pay debts.

intangible property. Personal property that does not have physical presence, such as the ownership interest in a corporation.

intellectual property. Legal rights to the products of the mind, such as writings, musical compositions, formulas, and designs.

L

legal person. An entity recognized by the state as a person apart from its members.

liability. The legal responsibility to pay for an injury.

licensing board. A government entity that grants permission to perform certain functions.

limited liability. Fixing the amount a person can be forced to pay for a legal event at a limited sum.

limited liability company. An artificial legal person set up to conduct a business owned and run by members.

limited liability partnership. An artificial legal person set up to conduct a business owned and run by members, which is set up for professionals such as attorneys or doctors.

limited partnership. A business that is owned by two or more persons, of which one or more is liable for the debts of the business and one or more has no liability for the debts.

M

management agreement. The document that controls the operation of a limited liability company that is managed by managers.

manager. A person who controls the operations of a limited liability company.

manager-managed LLC. A limited liability company that is controlled by one or more managers who are not all of the members of the company.

member. Person owning an interest in a limited liability company.

member-managed LLC. A limited liability company that is controlled by all of its members.

minority interest owners. The owners of an interest in an LLC who own less than a majority interest.

minutes. Records of the proceedings of business meetings.

N

natural person. A human being, as opposed to a legal person created by the law.

net worth. The value of a person or an entity after subtracting liabilities from assets.

nonprofit corporation. An entity recognized as a legal person that is set up to run an operation in which none of the profits are distributed to controlling members.

O

occupational license. A government-issued permit to transact business.

officers. Those persons who run the day-to-day affairs of the business; usually include a president, secretary, treasurer, and vice president.

operating agreement. A contract among members of a limited liability company spelling out how the company is to be run.

option. The right to buy stock at a future date, usually at a predetermined price.

organizational meeting. The meeting of the founders of a corporation or limited liability company in which the company is structured and ready to begin business.

P

partnership. A business formed by two or more persons.

par value. A value given to newly issued stock, which used to have legal significance, but now usually does not relate to anything except, in some states, taxation.

perpetual existence. Continuance of the business after a partner or owner dies.

personal liability. Being forced to pay for a liability out of personal funds rather than from limited company assets.

personal property. Any type of property other than land and the structures attached to it.

piercing the corporate veil. When a court ignores the corporate structure to hold the owners of the business liable.

professional association (P.A.). An entity recognized as a legal person that is set up to conduct a business of professionals, such as attorneys or doctors.

professional service corporation (P.C.). *See professional association.*

promissory note. A legal document in which a person promises to pay a sum of money.

promoters. Persons who start a business venture and usually offer interests for sale to investors.

proprietorship. A business that is owned by one person.

provisions. Terms of a legal document.

R

registered agent. A person who is designated by a limited liability company to receive legal papers for the company. (Also called resident agent in some states.)

registered office. A physical location where the registered agent of a limited liability company can receive legal papers for the company.

regulations. The former name of the operating agreement of a limited liability company.

S

S corporation. A corporation in which the profits are taxed to the shareholders.

securities. Interests in a business such as stock or bonds.

Securities and Exchange Commission (SEC). Government agency that regulates the buying and selling of stock.

shareholder. Person who owns stock in a corporation.

shareholder agreement. A contract among the owners of a corporation that spells out their rights.

shares. Units of stock in a corporation.

sole proprietorship. Type of business in which one person owns and has sole liability for the company.

stock. Ownership interests in a corporation.

stock certificate. Piece of paper used to represent shares of ownership; designates the number, class, and series of the stock issued.

T

tangible property. Physical personal property, such as desks and tables.

tax basis. The amount used as the cost of an item for tax purposes.

trademark. A name or symbol used to identify the source of goods or services.

transferability. The ability to sell shares of stock in a corporation.

U

undercapitalized. Not having enough money to soundly operate.

unemployment compensation. Payments to a former employee who was terminated from a job for a reason not based on his or her fault.

uniform business report. A form filed annually by an LLC in some states.

usury. Charging an interest rate higher than that allowed by law.

W

withholding. Money taken out of an employee's salary and remitted to the government.

Z

zoning. Laws that regulate the use of real estate.

Appendix

Contact Information and Special Requirements

The following pages contain a listing of each state's limited liability company laws and fees. Because the laws are constantly being changed by state legislatures, you should call before filing your papers to confirm the fees and other requirements. The phone numbers are provided for each state.

With the continued growth of the Internet, more and more state corporation divisions are making their forms, fees, and requirements available online. Some states have downloadable forms available, and some even allow you to search their entire database from the comfort of your home or office.

The current websites at the time of publication of this book are included for each state. However, the sites change constantly, so you may need to look a little deeper if your state's site has changed its address.

Note: *Not all states have a sample form.*

Alabama

Secretary of State
Corporations Division
P.O. Box 5616
Montgomery, AL 36103
334-242-5324

Website:
www.sos.state.al.us/business/
   corporations.cfm

LIMITED LIABILITY COMPANY

WHAT MUST BE FILED:

You must file the original and two copies of the Articles of Organization in the county where the LLC's registered office is located. The probate court judge will receive and record the original Articles. Within thirty days of filing, a completed report (provided by the secretary of state with the filing package) must be filed with the Judge of Probate ($5 filing fee).

ARTICLES OF ORGANIZATION SPECIAL REQUIREMENTS:

The Articles must set forth the rights, terms, and conditions to admit additional members, and, if given, the right by remaining members to continue business after dissociation.

STATUTES:

Code of Alabama, Title 10, Chapter 12, Alabama Limited Liability Company Act.

CORPORATION

WHAT MUST BE FILED:

You need to file the original and two copies of the Articles of Corporation in the county where the corporation's registered office is located.

ARTICLES REQUIREMENTS:

The minimum requirements for the Articles are as follows:

- the name of the corporation
- the period of duration
- the purpose of the corporation
- any provisions for the regulation of the internal affairs (including final liquidation)
- local and mailing address
- number of the directors constituting the initial board of directors and names and addresses of the initial directors
- name and address of each incorporator

STATUTE:

Alabama Code 10-3A-1 to 225

Alaska

Department of Commerce and
Economic Development
Division of B.S.C.
Attention: Corporation Section
P.O. Box 110808
Juneau, AK 99811
907-465-2530
Fax: 907-465-3257

Website:
www.commerce.state.ak.us/bsc/home.htm

LIMITED LIABILITY COMPANY

WHAT MUST BE FILED:

An original and an exact copy of the fill-in-the-blank Articles of Organization. The Articles should contain a statement that they are being filed under the provisions of the Alaska Limited Liability Act.

ARTICLES OF ORGANIZATION SPECIAL REQUIREMENTS:

The purpose of the LLC must be characterized with at least two S.I.C. code numbers which are listed in the chart on the next page.

STATUTES:

Alaska Statutes, Title 10, beginning with Section 50.010, Alaska Limited Liability Act.

CORPORATION

WHAT MUST BE FILED:

Print or type your documents in dark, legible print and file two copies of the Articles of Incorporation. Computer print must be high resolution, laser print quality, suitable for microfilming. Make sure your documents bear the original signatures and are both notarized. Enclose the filing fee. One copy will be returned to you for your records. Paper must be no larger than 8 by 11 inches.

ARTICLES REQUIREMENTS:

You must state the names, telephone numbers, and addresses of your initial (first) board of directors in Article 6. In Alaska there must be at least three incorporators who must be natural persons at least 19 years old. Enter the names and (business) addresses of these incorporators in Article 7. Make sure that your Articles are notarized. The Articles should contain a statement that they are being filed under the provisions of the Alaska Nonprofit Corporation Act (AS 10.20).

- the name of the corporation
- the period of duration, which may be perpetual
- the purpose or purposes for which the corporation is organized
- any provisions for the regulation of the internal affairs (including final liquidation)
- physical address of its initial registered office and the name of its initial registered agent
- number of the directors constituting the initial board of directors and names and addresses of persons who are to serve as the initial directors
- the name and address of each incorporator

STATUTE:

Alaska Statutes, Section 10.06.208-210

Arizona

Arizona Corporation Commission
1300 West Washington
Phoenix, AZ 85007
602-542-3026
800-345-5819 (Arizona residents only)
or
400 West Congress
Tucson, AZ 85701
520-628-6560

Website:
www.cc.state.az.us/corp/index.htm

LIMITED LIABILITY COMPANY

WHAT MUST BE FILED:

The original and one copy of the Articles of Organization must be filed with the Corporation Commission, copies will be returned if all requirements have been satisfied. DOMESTIC companies must publish a Notice of Filing. Within sixty days after filing, three consecutive publications of the Articles of Organization must be published in a newspaper of general circulation where the LLC has its place of business. Within ninety days after filing, an Affidavit evidencing the publication must also be filed with the Commission. This Affidavit will be supplied by the newspaper.

ARTICLES OF ORGANIZATION SPECIAL REQUIREMENTS:

The LLC must have a registered office and a statutory agent at a street address. The agent must sign the Articles or provide a consent to acceptance of appointment.

STATUTES:

Title 29, Chapter 4, Arizona Statutes (Arizona Limited Liability Company Act).

CORPORATION

WHAT MUST BE FILED:

Complete your Articles and file the original and two copies. Also fill in the Certificate of Disclosure and attach it to your Articles. Enclose the filing fee. After filing your Articles must be published within 60 days in a newspaper of general circulation in the county of the place of business in Arizona. There must be three consecutive publications of a copy of the approved Articles. Within 90 days of filing an affidavit evidencing the publication must be filed with the Commission.

ARTICLES REQUIREMENTS:

Enter one of the specific valid purposes for which a nonprofit corporation may be formed in Article 3.

In Article 5 and 6 you must enter the applicable Section number of of the IRS code under which your corporation plans to organize. Contact your local IRS office to obtain these numbers.

In Article 8 enter the name and business address of your initial statutory agent. This statutory agent has to sign the Articles on the bottom of the page.

Also complete your Certificate of Disclosure that has to be filed with your Articles. It contains information about your officers, directors, and anyone involved in the corporation.

STATUTE:

Arizona Revised Statutes, Section 10-2300

Arkansas

Secretary of State
Corporation Division
State Capitol
Room 256
Little Rock, AR 72201
501-682-5078
888-233-0325
(outside of the Little Rock area)
Website:
www.sosweb.state.ar.us/
corp_ucc_business.html

LIMITED LIABILITY COMPANY

WHAT MUST BE FILED:

File two copies of Articles of Organization. A file stamped copy will be returned to you after filing has been completed. Also file one copy of Limited Liability Company Franchise Tax registration form.

ARTICLES OF ORGANIZATION SPECIAL REQUIREMENTS:

Registered agent must sign acknowledgment and acceptance of the appointment.

If the management of the company is vested in managers this must be stated in the articles.

STATUTES:

Small Business Entity Tax Pass Through Act, Act 1003 of 1993, Ark. Code Annotated, beginning with Section 4-32-101.

CORPORATION

WHAT MUST BE FILED:

Complete both copies of the fill-in-the-blanks Articles and file them with the Secretary of State. Make sure that the Articles are signed by all incorporators.

ARTICLES REQUIREMENTS:

The minimum requirements for the Articles are as follows:

- the name of the corporation
- the determination whether the corporation shall be a public-benefit, a mutual-benefit or a religious corporation
- a statement whether or not the corporation will have members
- if applicable, provisions regarding the distribution of assets on dissolution
- the street address and the name of the corporation's initial registered office
- the address and signature of each incorporator

STATUTE:

Arkansas Code, Title 4, Sec. 28-206

California

Secretary of State
Corporations Division
1500 11th Street
Sacramento, CA 95814
916-657-5448
or
Statement of Information Unit
   (filings only)
P.O. Box 944230
Sacramento, CA 94244

Website:
www.ss.ca.gov/business/business.htm

LIMITED LIABILITY COMPANY

WHAT MUST BE FILED:

File only the original executed document together with the filing fee. A certified copy of the original document will be returned to you after filing.

ARTICLES OF ORGANIZATION SPECIAL REQUIREMENTS:

The Articles must be filed on California form LLC-1 and not a substitute. A form is on the next page.

STATUTES:

California Corporation Code, Section 17000-17062 (Beverly-Killea Limited Liability Company Act).

CORPORATION

WHAT MUST BE FILED:

Draft your own Articles accordingly to the applicable sample Articles provided by the state. The documents must be typed in black ink on one side of the paper only. To avoid the initial annual franchise tax of $800 complete the application form for exemption from franchise tax (form 3500), enclose all attachments called for in the instructions, and file this application together with the original and four copies of your Articles. Also enclose the $25 application filing fee, the state filing fee, and a self-addressed envelope. The Secretary of State will certify two copies without charge. Any additional copies will be certified upon request and payment of $8 per copy.

ARTICLES REQUIREMENTS:

Articles must have the following minimum contents:

- the corporate name
- the general purpose (Mutual Benefit Corporation, Public Benefit Corporation, Religious Corporation) and the specific purpose of the corporation
- name and California street address of the initial agent (post office box alone is not acceptable)
- signature and typed name (directly below the signature) of at least one incorporator
- if directors are stated in the Articles, each named person must acknowledge and sign the Articles
- special statements required to be included in the Articles to get the tax exemption (only where applicable—please contact the Franchise Tax Board under the address typed below)

STATUTE:

California Code, Nonprofit Corporation Law, Public Benefit Corporations, Section 5122

Colorado

Secretary of State
Business Division
1560 Broadway, Suite 200
Denver, CO 80202
303-894-2200

Website:
www.sos.state.co.us/pubs/
    business/main.htm

LIMITED LIABILITY COMPANY

WHAT MUST BE FILED:

You must file the typed original and one copy of the Articles of Organization with the secretary of state. You need to include a self-addressed envelope.

ARTICLES OF ORGANIZATION SPECIAL REQUIREMENTS:

No special requirements.

STATUTES:

Colorado Limited Liability Company Act, Colorado Revised Statutes, beginning with Section 7-80-101.

CORPORATION

WHAT MUST BE FILED:

Make a copy of the fill-in-the-blanks Articles and complete both documents by typing them in black ink. File both originals and enclose the filing fee. Include a typed or machine printed self-addressed envelope.

ARTICLES REQUIREMENTS:

The minimum requirements for a Colorado nonprofit corporation are as follows:

- the corporate name
- the name and street address of the corporation's registered agent and office
- the name and address of each incorporator
- a statement whether or not the corporation will have members
- provisions regarding distribution of assets upon dissolution
- the number of directors your corporation shall have

Make sure that each incorporator listed signs the Articles.

STATUTE:

Colorado Revised Statutes, Chapter 7–122 of the Colorado Nonprofit Corporation Act

Connecticut

Secretary of State
Commercial Recording Division
30 Trinity Street
Hartford, CT 06106
860-509-6002
860-509-6001

Website:
www.sots.state.ct.us/Business/
   BusinessMain.html

LIMITED LIABILITY COMPANY

WHAT MUST BE FILED:

Single copy of Articles of Organization must be filed with the secretary of state. You will receive a mailing receipt. Copies are at additional charge (see below).

ARTICLES OF ORGANIZATION SPECIAL REQUIREMENTS:

Statutory agent must sign.

STATUTES:

Connecticut Limited Liability Company Act, Pub. Act 93-267, Connecticut Statutes, Title 34.

CORPORATION

WHAT MUST BE FILED:

Type or print your Certificate of Incorporation in black ink. File only the original together with the filing fee.

ARTICLES REQUIREMENTS:

In Article 2 check the appropriate box whether your corporation shall have members and what rights they shall have. Enter the name and address of your registered agent in Article 3 and make sure the agent signs the Acceptance of appointment.

As a nonprofit, nonstock corporation the purpose of your corporation may be "to engage in any lawful act or activity for which corporations may be formed under the Connecticut Revised Non stock corporation Act" (Article 4).

STATUTE:

Connecticut General Statutes, Nonstock Corporations, Sec. 33-427

Delaware

State of Delaware
Division of Corporations
John G. Townsend Building
401 Federal Street, Suite 4
Dover, DE 19901
  or (for regular mail)
P.O. Box 898
Dover, DE 19903
302-739-3073

Website:
www.state.de.us/corp

LIMITED LIABILITY COMPANY

WHAT MUST BE FILED:

The original and one copy of the Certificate of Formation must be filed with the secretary of state. The documents must be submitted in the U.S. letter size (8.5"x11") with certain margins and must be either typed, printed, or written in black ink.

ARTICLES OF ORGANIZATION SPECIAL REQUIREMENTS:

The document is called a "Certificate of Formation" in Delaware and has only three requirements, the name, address of the registered office, and name of registered agent.

STATUTES:

Title 6, Commerce and Trade, Chapter 18, Limited Liability Company Act.

CORPORATION

WHAT MUST BE FILED:

Complete the fill-in-the-blanks form Certificate of Incorporation for "nonstock corporations." Print or type your documents in black ink and submit any additional documents in the US letter size 8.5"x11". File the original Certificate of Formation and one exact copy. Enclose the filing fee.

ARTICLES REQUIREMENTS:

Nonprofit corporations must add, "This Corporation shall be a nonprofit corporation" in the third Article.

In Article 4 you are asked to state your membership conditions but you can also leave that to be regulated by your Bylaws.

STATUTE:

Delaware Code Annotated, Title 8, Sec. 102

District of Columbia

Department of Consumer and
  Regulatory Affairs
Corporation Division
941 North Capital Street NE
Washington, D.C. 20002
202-442-4400

Website:
http://dcra.dc.gov/dcra/site/default.asp

LIMITED LIABILITY COMPANY

WHAT MUST BE FILED:

You must file two signed originals of Articles of Organization. Attach the written consent of the registered agent.

ARTICLES OF ORGANIZATION SPECIAL REQUIREMENTS:

The registered agent must consent to his appointment.

If a general or limited partnership converts to a limited liability company, the former name and fact of conversion must be stated Articles of Organization.

STATUTES:

Title 29, Chapter 10 of the District of Columbia Code (D.C. Limited Liability Company Act of 1994).

CORPORATION

WHAT MUST BE FILED:

Draft your own Articles accordingly to the instructions and the sample Articles given by the State. Use plain bond paper, either U.S. letter or legal size. Submit two originally signed and notarized sets of Articles.

ARTICLES REQUIREMENTS:

The minimum requirements for the Articles are as follows:

- the name of the corporation
- the period of duration (this can be perpetual or a specific period)
- a specific purpose for which the corporation is organized
- a statement whether the corporation shall have members
- if your corporation shall have members, the number of classes of members and the different qualifications and rights of the members of each class
- the manner in which directors shall be elected or appointed and a statement of which class of members shall have the right to elect directors
- a provision of the regulation of the internal affairs of the corporation
- the name of the initial registered agent and the address of the initial registered office
- the number of initial directors the corporation shall have and their names and addresses
- the names and addresses of each incorporator (incorporators must be at least 21 years of age)

STATUTE:

D.C. Code, Title 29, Chapter 5

Florida

Secretary of State
Division of Corporations
P.O. Box 6327
Tallahassee, FL 32314
800-755-5111

Website:
www.dos.state.fl.us/doc/index.html

LIMITED LIABILITY COMPANY

WHAT MUST BE FILED:

Unless this material has been included in your articles, one original copy of the Articles of Organization must be filed along with the Certificate of Designation of Registered Agent. An Affidavit of Membership and Contributions must also be filed unless this information is included in your articles. If you include a copy of the articles, it will be date-stamped and returned. Otherwise, you will receive an acknowledgement letter.

ARTICLES OF ORGANIZATION SPECIAL REQUIREMENTS:

If the Limited Liability Company is to be managed by one or more managers, a statement that the company is to be a manager-managed company needs to be included in the Articles.

An acceptance by the registered agent and an affidavit of membership and contributions must be either included in the Articles or on a separate form.

STATUTES:

Title 36, Chapter 608, Florida Statutes (Florida Limited Liability Company Act).

AUTHOR'S NOTE: *As this books goes to press, major revisions of the Florida Act are pending before the legislature and may become effective January 1, 2008.*

CORPORATION

WHAT MUST BE FILED:

Complete the sample Articles and file the original and one copy. Also complete the transmittal letter provided by the state and attach it to your Articles. Enclose the correct filing fee.

ARTICLES REQUIREMENTS:

The minimum requirements for the Articles are as follows:

- the name of the corporation
- the principal place of business and mailing address of the corporation
- a specific purpose for which the corporation is formed
- a statement, in which manner the directors are elected or appointed
- the name and Florida street address of your initial registered agent—make sure your registered agent signs the Articles in the space on the bottom page
- the name and signature of each incorporator

STATUTE:

Florida Statutes, Chapter 617

Georgia

Secretary of State
2 Martin Luther King, Jr. Drive, S.E.
Suite 315, West Tower
Atlanta, GA 30334
404-656-2817

Website:
www.sos.state.ga.us/corporations

LIMITED LIABILITY COMPANY

WHAT MUST BE FILED:

You must file the original and one copy of the Articles of Organization and attach the Transmittal form provided by the State.

ARTICLES OF ORGANIZATION SPECIAL REQUIREMENTS:

The name of the company must be in the Articles. If the company is to be managed by someone other than the members, a clause should be added indicating who are the managers. Other information, such as the address of the company and registered agent, is to be included on the "Transmittal Information" sheet.

The Articles must be signed by all members.

STATUTES:

Title 14, Chapter 11 of the Official Code of Georgia Annotated.

CORPORATION

WHAT MUST BE FILED:

Draft your own Articles accordingly to the guidelines given by the state. Submit the original and one exact copy. Also fill in the "Transmittal Information" form and attach it to the Articles. Enclose the filing fee.

Note that all corporations have to publish a notice of intent to incorporate in the official legal newspaper of the county in which the registered office of the corporation is located (the Clerk of Superior Court will give you advice). You must forward your notice of intent together with a $40 publication fee directly to the newspaper on the next business day after filing your Articles. A sample notice of incorporation is included in the instructions how to draft your Articles.

ARTICLES REQUIREMENTS:

The Articles must contain the following minimum:

- the name of the corporation
- a statement that the corporation is organized pursuant to the Georgia Nonprofit Corporation Code
- the name of the registered agent and the street address of its office in Georgia (a post office box address alone is not acceptable)
- the name and address of each incorporator
- a statement whether the corporation shall have members
- the mailing address of the corporation
- a signature of one of the incorporators named in the Articles

STATUTE:

Georgia Code Annotated, Title 14-2-120, Sec. 2702

Hawaii

Business Registration Division
Department of Commerce
and Consumer Affairs
P.O. Box 40
Honolulu, HI 96810
808-586-2744

Website:
www.hawaii.gov/dcca

LIMITED LIABILITY COMPANY

WHAT MUST BE FILED:

You must file the original and one copy of the Articles of Organization.

ARTICLES OF ORGANIZATION SPECIAL REQUIREMENTS:

The Articles should state that the members are not liable for the debts of the company under Section 428-303(c) Hawaii Statutes.

If there are managers their names and residence addresses must be included, otherwise the name and residence addresses of the members must be listed.

STATUTES:

Title 23A, Chapter 428, Hawaii Revised Statutes.

CORPORATION

WHAT MUST BE FILED:

Complete both copies and file them with the Secretary of State. Enclose the filing fee.

ARTICLES REQUIREMENTS:

The Articles shall set forth the following minimum:

- the name of the corporation
- the address of the corporation's office
- the purpose for which the corporation is organized
- the names and street addresses of the initial directors
- the names and street addresses of the initial officer
- a statement whether the corporation shall have members
- the signature of each incorporator

STATUTE:

Hawaii Revised Statutes, Title 23, Section 415B-34

Idaho

Secretary of State
Attn: Commercial Division
P.O. Box 83720
Boise, ID 83720
208-334-2301

Website:
www.idsos.state.id.us/corp/corindex.htm

LIMITED LIABILITY COMPANY

WHAT MUST BE FILED:

You must file two completed originals. The fill-in-the-blank forms must be typed, if not typed or if the attachments are not included, there is an additional $20 fee for filing.

If you have questions about the correct filing, you can call the secretary of state's office at 208-334-2301.

ARTICLES OF ORGANIZATION SPECIAL REQUIREMENTS:

The address of the registered office may not be a P.O. Box, but must be a physical address in Idaho. The registered agent must sign the articles. If the management shall be vested in managers, at least one manager has to sign the Articles.

The name and address of at least one manager or member must be included.

STATUTES:

Title 53, Chapter 6, Idaho Limited Liability Company Act.

CORPORATION

WHAT MUST BE FILED:

Fill-in forms are provided by the state. File the original and one exact copy together with the filing fee.

ARTICLES REQUIREMENTS:

The Articles must contain the following minimum requirements:

- the name of the corporation
- the purpose for which the corporation is formed (this can be to transact any and all lawful activity for which a nonprofit corporation can be formed)
- the names and addresses of the initial directors
- the name of the initial registered agent and the address of the registered office
- the name and address of each incorporator
- a statement whether or not the corporation shall have members
- any other provision regarding the distribution of assets on dissolution

Make sure that each incorporator signs the Articles.

STATUTE:

Idaho Statutes, Title 30, Chapter 3, Idaho Nonprofit Corporation Act

Illinois

Springfield Office:
Secretary of State
Business Services Dept.
Michael J. Howlett Bldg.
501 S. 2nd Street
Room 328
Springfield, IL 62756
217-782-6961

Chicago Office:
Secretary of State
Business Services Dept.
69 W. Washington
Suite 1240
Chicago, IL 60602
312-793-3380

Website:
www.cyberdriveillinois.com/departments/
business_services/home.html

LIMITED LIABILITY COMPANY

WHAT MUST BE FILED:

File the original and one copy of the signed Articles of Organization form. The form must be typed.

ARTICLES OF ORGANIZATION SPECIAL REQUIREMENTS:

If there are managers, their names and residence addresses must be included; otherwise the name and residence addresses of the members must be listed.

In Article 6 you are asked for the business purpose by (SIC) code. However, the statute states that the purpose can be "any or all lawful business."

STATUTES:

The Illinois Limited Liability Company Act, 805 ILCS 180.

CORPORATION

WHAT MUST BE FILED:

Type or print your documents in black ink and file the original and one exact copy. Enclose the filing fee.

After you receive the certificate and your file stamped Articles from the Secretary of State, you must file them with the office of the Recorder of Deeds of the county in which your registered office is located. The recording must be within 15 days after receiving your certificate.

ARTICLES REQUIREMENTS:

The purpose for which the corporation is formed (Article 4) must be a specific purpose and may not be too general or broad. A list of allowable purposes can be found in the booklet provided by the state (see page 3 of the booklet). Also in Article 4 check the appropriate box whether your corporation shall be a Condominium Association or whether your corporation shall be Cooperative Housing or Homeowner's Association.

STATUTE:

Illinois Compiled Statutes Chapter 805, Act 105, 1992, The General Not For Profit Corporation Act of 1986

Indiana

Secretary of State
302 W. Washington, Room E018
Indianapolis, IN 46204
317-232-6576

Website:
www.in.gov/sos/business/index.html

LIMITED LIABILITY COMPANY

WHAT MUST BE FILED:

File original and two copies of the Articles of Organization with the secretary of state. Enclose the filing fee.

ARTICLES OF ORGANIZATION SPECIAL REQUIREMENTS:

No unusual clauses are required.

STATUTES:

Indiana Code Title 23, Chapter 18.

CORPORATION

WHAT MUST BE FILED:

Type or print all three copies of the fill-in-the-blanks forms and file them with the Secretary of State. Enclose the filing fee.

ARTICLES REQUIREMENTS:

In Article 3 check the appropriate box whether the corporation is a public benefit, a religious, or a mutual benefit corporation. Also check in Article 5 whether the corporation will have members. Make sure that the Articles are signed by each incorporator.

STATUTE:

Indiana Code Sec. 23-17, Indiana Nonprofit Corporation Act of 1991

Iowa

Secretary of State
Corporations Division
Lucas Building, 1st Floor
321 East 12th Street
Des Moines, IA 50319
515-281-5204

Website:
www.sos.state.ia.us/business

LIMITED LIABILITY COMPANY

WHAT MUST BE FILED:

File only the original of your Articles of Organization. The document must be typed or printed in black ink. If all requirements are met, the Articles will be returned as filed.

ARTICLES OF ORGANIZATION SPECIAL REQUIREMENTS:

The principal office must be listed. (This may be the same as the registered office, but doesn't need to be.)

STATUTES:

Chapter 490A, Iowa Codes, Iowa Limited Liability Company Act.

CORPORATION

WHAT MUST BE FILED:

Draft your own Articles of Incorporation accordingly to the guidelines and Section 504A.29 of the Iowa Nonprofit Corporation Act. See "Articles Requirements" below for details. Deliver the original document and one exact copy together with the filing fee.

ARTICLES REQUIREMENTS:

The Articles must include the following minimum:

- the name of the corporation and the Chapter of the Code under which incorporated
- if you want your corporation to be formed for a limited time the period of duration, skip that if it shall be perpetual
- the purpose for which the organization is organized (must be a charitable, literary, educational, or scientific purpose)
- any provisions that set forth the regulation of the internal affairs of the corporation, including provisions of the distribution of assets upon dissolution
- the name of the registered agent and the address of the initial registered office
- the number and the names and addresses of the initial directors
- if applicable, any provision limiting any of the corporate powers
- the date on which the corporate existence shall begin (not more than ninety days in the future)—you can skip this, your corporation will then exist from the date the state issues the certificate of incorporation
- the name and address of each incorporator

Make sure that the person executing the documents signs and states his or her name and capacity in which he or she signs.

STATUTE:

Iowa Code Sec. 504A.29

Kansas

Secretary of State
Corporation Division
Memorial Hall, 1st Floor
120 SW 10th Avenue
Topeka, KS 66612
785-296-4564

Website:
www.kssos.org/business/business.html

LIMITED LIABILITY COMPANY

WHAT MUST BE FILED:

The Articles of Organization must be signed by the person forming the organization or by any member or manager. You must file the original signed copy and one duplicate, which may either be a signed or conformed copy. Enclose the filing fee.

ARTICLES OF ORGANIZATION SPECIAL REQUIREMENTS:

The address of its registered office and the address of the registered agent for service of process must be the same, but the agent can be the LLC itself.

If the members have the right to admit additional members, this must be included in the Articles along with the terms and conditions of the admission.

If the remaining members have the right to continue the business upon any event which terminates the continued membership of a member of the limited liability company, this must be included.

The names and addresses of the managers or if none, names and addresses of the members must be included.

STATUTES:

Kansas Statutes Annotated, beginning with Section 17-7601.

CORPORATION

WHAT MUST BE FILED:

Complete the fill-in-the-blanks form and file the original and one exact copy. Note that the Articles of Incorporation must be notarized. Enclose the filing fee.

ARTICLES REQUIREMENTS:

The purpose your corporation is formed for must be stated in Article 3, a general statement that the purpose is to "engage in any lawful act or activity for which nonprofit corporations may be organized under the Kansas General Corporation Code" is sufficient. You should check with the IRS prior to filing whether your purpose must be specific one.

If you want to apply for the federal tax exempt status you must check the "No" box in Article 4 to make clear that your corporation won't issue capital stock.

Enter the names and mailing addresses of the persons serving as initial directors until the first annual meeting. Make sure the incorporator (minimum of one) signs the Articles.

STATUTE:

Kansas Statutes Annotated, Sec. 17-6002, Corporations

Kentucky

Commonwealth of Kentucky
Office of the Secretary of State
700 Capitol Avenue, Suite 152
Frankfort, KY 40601
502-564-3490

Website:
www.sos.state.ky.us

LIMITED LIABILITY COMPANY

WHAT MUST BE FILED:

File your typewritten (or printed) and signed Articles original accompanied by two exact copies. If the company will be managed by managers, the documents must be signed by the managers, or by a least one member. The person signing the document has to state the capacity in which she or he signs.

ARTICLES OF ORGANIZATION SPECIAL REQUIREMENTS:

The registered agent must consent to his or her appointment by signing the Articles.

STATUTES:

Chapter 275 Kentucky Statutes, Kentucky Limited Liability Company Act.

CORPORATION

WHAT MUST BE FILED:

The Articles must be typewritten or printed, and signed by an incorporator if no director has been selected. File the original and two exact copies of your Articles and enclose the correct filing fee. The Secretary of State will return two "filed" stamped copies to your registered agent's office.

ARTICLES REQUIREMENTS:

The minimum requirements for the Articles are:

- the corporate name
- the purpose or purposes for which the corporation is organized
- the name of the initial registered agent and the address of its office
- the mailing address of the corporation's principal office
- the number of the initial directors and the names and mailing addresses of these persons
- the name and mailing address of each incorporator
- any provisions for distribution of assets on dissolution or final liquidation of your corporation

STATUTE:

Kentucky Revised Statutes, Chapter 273

Louisiana

Secretary of State
Corporations Division
P.O. Box 94125
Baton Rouge, LA 70804
225-925-4704

Website:
www.sos.louisiana.gov/comm/corp/
    corp-index.htm

LIMITED LIABILITY COMPANY

WHAT MUST BE FILED:

Complete both the Articles and the Initial Report. Both documents must be signed by the people organizing the LLC and both must be notarized. File only the originals and enclose the filing fee.

ARTICLES OF ORGANIZATION SPECIAL REQUIREMENTS:

Articles of Organization must be notarized. They must be accompanied by form 973 "Initial Report" which must be signed by all persons who signed the Articles of Organization and the registered agent and be notarized.

STATUTES:

Louisiana Revised Statutes beginning with Section 12:1301.

CORPORATION

WHAT MUST BE FILED:

To obtain a federal tax identification number call the IRS at 901-546-3920 prior to filing your Articles.

Complete the fill-in-the-blanks form provided by the state. Make sure that your registered agent signs the affidavit on the bottom of the second page. Both Articles and affidavit have to be notarized. File only the original and enclose the filing fee.

Within 30 days after filing your Articles, a multiple original or a copy certified by the Secretary of State and a copy of the Certificate of Incorporation must be filed with the office of the recorder of mortgages in the parish where the corporation's registered office is located.

ARTICLES REQUIREMENTS:

In Article 2 check the first box if you do not want the purpose of the corporation to be limited.

If you want to apply for the federal tax-exempt status you must check "Non-stock basis" in Article 9 to make clear that your corporation does not issue stock. You then have to fill in Article 10, characterizing the qualifications which must be met to be a member of your corporation.

STATUTE:

Louisiana Revised Statutes, Chapter 12:203

Maine

Secretary of State
Bureau of Corporations, Elections,
and Commissions
101 State House Station
Augusta, ME 04333
207-624-7736

Website:
www.state.me.us/sos/cec/corp/corp.htm

LIMITED LIABILITY COMPANY

WHAT MUST BE FILED:

File the typewritten or printed original Articles of Organization. If the registered agent does not sign the Articles, he or she must sign the Acceptance of Appointment as Registered Agent.

ARTICLES OF ORGANIZATION SPECIAL REQUIREMENTS:

If there are managers, a statement to that effect must be included along with the minimum and maximum number of managers. If they have been selected, their names and addresses must be included.

STATUTES:

Maine Revised Statutes Title 31, Chapter 13, beginning with Section 601-762.

CORPORATION

WHAT MUST BE FILED:

Type or print your Articles in black ink. Make sure all your documents are dated by month, day and year and all bear original signatures. File the original and attach the completed Acceptance of Appoint-ment as registered agent. Make sure to enclose the correct filing fee.

ARTICLES REQUIREMENTS:

If you do not want the purpose for which your corporation is formed to be limited, just leave Article 2 blank, so that the corporation is organized for all purposes permitted under the law. Enter the number of your initial directors and of the directors to be elected on your first meeting in Article 4 and check the appropriate box in Article 5, whether or not your corporation shall have members.

Articles 6 and 7 are optional. Check with the IRS prior to filing your Articles, if your corporation has to meet the requirements stated in Article 7.

STATUTE:

Maine Revisted Statutes Annotated, Title 13-B

Maryland

State Department of
Assessments and Taxation
Corporate Charter Division
301 West Preston Street, Room 801
Baltimore, MD 21201
410-767-1340
888-246-5941 (in state)

Website:
www.dat.state.md.us/sdatweb/
sdatforms.html

LIMITED LIABILITY COMPANY

WHAT MUST BE FILED:

Type or print your Articles, handwritten documents are not accepted. Submit the signed original for filing. If you want a certified copy, add an additional $6 plus $1 to your filing check for each additional page.

ARTICLES OF ORGANIZATION SPECIAL REQUIREMENTS:

No special items are required in the Articles, but they request that the return address of the Articles be clearly noted.

STATUTES:

Maryland Code, Corps. & Ass'ns., beginning with Section 4A-101.

CORPORATION

WHAT MUST BE FILED:

Your documents must be typed. File only the original and enclose the filing fee.

ARTICLES REQUIREMENTS:

Characterize the purpose for which the corporation is formed with one or two sentences in Article 3 and make sure the purpose is charitable, religious, educational, or scientific.

Enter the minimum and maximum number of directors your corporation shall have and give the name and address of the initial director(s) in the space below.

STATUTE:

Annotated Code of Maryland, Corporations and Associations, Sec. 2-104

Massachusetts

Secretary of the Commonwealth
Corporations Division
One Ashburton Place, 17th Floor
Boston, MA 02108
617-727-9640

Website:
www.sec.state.ma.us/cor

LIMITED LIABILITY COMPANY

WHAT MUST BE FILED:

File the original signed copy together with a photocopy or a duplicate original. The documents must be signed either by the person forming the LLC, by any manager (if there are any), or by a trustee.

ARTICLES OF ORGANIZATION SPECIAL REQUIREMENTS:

If available, the Federal Employer Identification Number (FEIN) should be included on the articles. This is obtained by filing IRS form SS-4 (form 3 in appendix C). If the number is needed quickly it can be obtained over the phone (404-455-2360), but you must have form SS-4 completed and in front of you.

If there are managers, their names and residence addresses must be included. If the managers' business addresses are different from that of the LLC, their addresses must be listed.

If there is anyone other than a manager who is authorized to execute papers filed with the Corporations Division, their name and business must be included. If there are no managers, at least one member's name and business address must be listed.

STATUTES:

Annotated Laws of massachusetts, Title 22, Chapter 156C, Massachusetts Limited Liability Act.

CORPORATION

WHAT MUST BE FILED:

Complete the sample Articles and file the original document with the Secretary of State.

ARTICLES REQUIREMENTS:

The purpose your corporation is formed for can be explained in simple language in Article 2, but if you want to apply for the tax-exempt status, characterize that purpose more specifically in Article 4. Check with the IRS for what requirements must be met to receive the tax-exemption.

STATUTE:

Massachusetts General Laws, Chapter 180

Michigan

Michigan Department of Commerce
Corporation and Securities Bureau
Corporation Division
P.O. Box 30054
Lansing, MI 48909
517-241-6470

Website:
www.michigan.gov/cis

LIMITED LIABILITY COMPANY

WHAT MUST BE FILED:

The Articles must be typed or filled in with black ink. Either form C&S 700 must be used for the Articles or it should accompany your Articles.

If you prefer the fax filing procedure, fill in the "ELF Application" form (you must provide your Visa/Mastercard number here), the cover sheet, and check the fax filing checklist (provided by the State).

ARTICLES OF ORGANIZATION SPECIAL REQUIREMENTS:

The Articles of Organization must be either on form C&S 700 (which has specific spaces for filing number, date received and return address) or a "comparable document." If you have drafted your own articles, they suggest that you attach C&S 700 as a cover sheet.

STATUTES:

Act 23 of the Public Acts of 1993, Michigan Limited Liability Company Act, or Michigan Compiled Laws, beginning with Section 450.4101.

CORPORATION

WHAT MUST BE FILED:

Complete the fill-in-the-blanks form by typing or printing legibly in black ink. File only the original document together with the correct filing fee.

ARTICLES REQUIREMENTS:

Characterize the purpose for which your corporation is formed. This purpose must be specific. A general statement is not sufficient.

Complete either Article III (2) or III (3) depending on whether or not your corporation will issue stock. If you want to apply for the federal tax-exempt status your corporation will be on a non stock basis.

Note that except for educational corporations, which must have at least three incorporators, your corporation must only have one incorporator.

STATUTE:

Michigan Compiled Laws, Sec. 21.197/202

Minnesota

Secretary of State
Division of Corporations
180 State Office Building
100 Reverend Dr. Martin Luther King Jr.
  Boulevard
St. Paul, MN 55155
651-296-2803
877-551-6767 (greater Minnesota)

Website:
www.sos.state.mn.us

LIMITED LIABILITY COMPANY

WHAT MUST BE FILED:

Type or print your articles in black ink (illegible articles will be returned). Must have original signatures.

ARTICLES OF ORGANIZATION SPECIAL REQUIREMENTS:

Registered agent is optional. SIC code should be provided from the following list of 19 choices:

00. Agriculture, Forestry, Fishing
10. Mining
15. Construction
20. Manufacturing—Non-Durable Goods
35. Manufacturing—Durable Goods
40. Transportation
48. Communications
49. Utilities
50. Wholesale trade
54. Retail—Non-Durable Goods
57. Retail—Durable Goods
60. Finance, Insurance, Real Estate
73. Business Services
80. Health Services
83. Social Services
86. Membership Organizations
87. Engineering and Management Services
89. Other Services
90. Other

If your LLC owns, leases, or has interest in agricultural land as described in M.S. Section 500.24 this should be stated.

STATUTES:

Chapter 322 B Minnesota Statutes.

CORPORATION

WHAT MUST BE FILED:

Print or type your document(s) legibly in black ink. File only the original.

ARTICLES REQUIREMENTS:

Check the "Nonprofit Corporation" box at the top of your Articles. Enter the name of your initial registered agent and the address of its registered office in Article 2. Make sure that each incorporator (minimum of one) signs the Articles.

STATUTE:

Minnesota Statutes Annotated Sec. 317A.111

Mississippi

Secretary of State
Business Services Division
P.O. Box 136
Jackson, MS 39205
601-359-1633
800-256-3494

Website:
www.sos.state.ms.us/busserv/corp/
corporations.asp

LIMITED LIABILITY COMPANY

WHAT MUST BE FILED:

For computer legibility make sure you fill in the forms exactly as described in the instructions. File the original copy signed by the person forming the limited liability company. Enclose the filing fee.

ARTICLES OF ORGANIZATION SPECIAL REQUIREMENTS:

The Mississippi form is bar coded and meant to be machine-readable. Using their form will speed up your filing, but it is not required.

You need to provide the Federal Employer Identification Number (F.E.I.N.), which must be obtained prior to filing. This is obtained by filing IRS form SS-4 (form 3 in appendix C). If the number is needed quickly it can be obtained over the phone (404-455-2360), but you must have form SS-4 completed and in front of you.

The name of the company is limited to 120 characters on the bar-coded form, and some other information is limited in the number of characters allowed.

STATUTES:

Mississippi Code beginning with Section 79-29-101.

CORPORATION

WHAT MUST BE FILED:

Complete the fill-in-the-blanks form exactly as described in the instructions. File only the original and enclose the filing fee. Attach the completed statement that your corporation is organized only for the purposes that will be recognized for the tax exemption.

ARTICLES REQUIREMENTS:

In Article 4 nonprofit corporations can determine the period of duration, enter either a certain number of years or check "perpetual."

Give the name and address of each incorporator in Article 7.

STATUTE:

Mississippi Code Annotated Sec. 79-11-137

Missouri

Corporations Division
P.O. Box 778
Jefferson City, MO 65102
573-751-4153
866-223-6535

Website:
www.sos.mo.gov/business/corporations/
Default.asp

LIMITED LIABILITY COMPANY

WHAT MUST BE FILED:

File the completed Articles in duplicate. Sign each copy and enclose the filing fee. If your documents conform to the filing provisions, the secretary will return the duplicate copy to the organizer.

ARTICLES OF ORGANIZATION SPECIAL REQUIREMENTS:

Missouri Statutes do not include any unusual requirements for the Articles.

STATUTES:

Chapter 347 Missouri Revised Statutes.

CORPORATION

WHAT MUST BE FILED:

Complete the fill-in-the-blanks forms and file your Articles in duplicate. Make sure both documents are originally signed. Enclose the filing fee.

ARTICLES REQUIREMENTS:

If you want to apply for the tax exempt status, make sure to meet the special requirements listed in the separate instructions. These requirements are as follows:

- the purpose for which the corporation is formed (Article 8) must be a charitable, educational, religious, or scientific one (to meet the state's requirements you also have to indicate exactly what your corporation is doing)
- the net income of the corporation may not distributed to the member, directors, or other private persons except for reasonable compensation for services rendered
- the corporation may not take part in any political or legislative activities
- upon the dissolution of the corporation the remaining assets must be distributed either for the corporation's purposes or to any other similar corporation qualified as exempt organizations

STATUTE:

Missouri Revised Statutes, Chapter 347

Montana

Secretary of State
P.O. Box 202801
Helena, MT 59620
406-444-3665

Website:
www.sos.state.mt.us/css/BSB/Contents.asp

LIMITED LIABILITY COMPANY

WHAT MUST BE FILED:

File the original and one copy of your signed Articles and enclose the correct filing fee.

"Priority filing" ensures twenty-four hour turn-around for an additional fee.

ARTICLES OF ORGANIZATION SPECIAL REQUIREMENTS:

The registered agent must sign the Articles. If there are managers, their names and residence addresses must be included; otherwise, the name and residence addresses of the members must be listed.

STATUTES:

Title 35, Chapter 8, Montana Code Annotated.

CORPORATION

WHAT MUST BE FILED:

First you have to check if the chosen name of your corporation is available. For this information you have to call the office of the Secretary of State. Then file the fill-in-the-blanks Articles and make a copy of the completed Articles. Mail both documents to the Secretary of State and enclose the filing fee.

ARTICLES REQUIREMENTS:

Your Articles have to include at least the following contents:

- corporate name
- name and address of the registered agent and office in Montana
- name and address of each incorporator
- the specific purpose of the corporation (because the Internal Revenue Service requires specific language in order to qualify for nonprofit tax status it is advised that you contact the IRS)
- a statement whether the corporation will have members
- distribution of assets in the case of dissolution

STATUTE:

Montana Revised Statutes Sec. 35-2-202

Nebraska

Corporations Division
P.O. Box 94608
Lincoln, NE 68509
402-471-4079

Website:
www.sos.state.ne.us/business/corp_serv

LIMITED LIABILITY COMPANY

WHAT MUST BE FILED:

Two copies of the Articles.

ARTICLES OF ORGANIZATION SPECIAL REQUIREMENTS:

Must include the cash and property contributed as stated capital and events which will trigger the contribution of additional capital, if any. All managers' names and addresses, or if managed by members, all members' names and addresses must be listed.

Duration cannot exceed thirty years.

STATUTES:

Chapter 21, beginning with Section 2601 Nebraska Limited Liability Company Act.

CORPORATION

WHAT MUST BE FILED:

You have to draw your own Articles. Follow the instructions given by the state. The document must be executed by an incorporator. The executing incorporator has to state her or his name and capacity ("incorporator") beneath or opposite the signature. Send the original and one copy to the secretary of state for filing. Make sure that you enclose the correct filing fee.

ARTICLES REQUIREMENTS:

Articles have to include the following basic contents:

- the corporate name
- a statement about the general purpose of the corporation (public benefit corporation, mutual-benefit corporation or religious corporation)
- street address (post office box is not acceptable) of corporation's registered office and the name of its initial registered agent at that office
- name and street address of each incorporator
- a statement whether or not the corporation will have members
- provisions not consistent with the law regarding the distribution of assets on dissolution

STATUTE:

Nebraska Revised Statutes Chapter 21-1905 et seq.

Nevada

Secretary of State
202 North Carson Street
Carson City, NV 89701
775-684-5708

Website:
www.sos.state.nv.us

LIMITED LIABILITY COMPANY

WHAT MUST BE FILED:

File the original and as many copies of it as you want certified and returned to you. The articles must be acknowledged by a notary. Enclose the filing fee with an additional $20 for each certification.

ARTICLES OF ORGANIZATION SPECIAL REQUIREMENTS:

If the company is to be managed by managers, their names and addresses must be included, otherwise the names and addresses of the members must be included.

STATUTES:

Chapter 86 Nevada Revised Statutes.

CORPORATION

WHAT MUST BE FILED:

Type or print your Articles in black ink only. File the original and as many copies as you want to be certified and returned to you. Note that you must at least keep one certified copy in the office of your resident agent. Make sure that each incorporator's signature is notarized.

ARTICLES REQUIREMENTS:

Enter the name and address of the initial resident agent in Article 2 and make sure that agent signs the certificate of acceptance on the bottom of the page.

To characterize the purpose for which the corporation is formed in accordance to the IRS requirements check with the IRS prior to filing.

Give the names and addresses of the initial Governing Board in Article 4. Do not forget that each incorporator's signature must be notarized.

STATUTE:

Nevada Revised Statutes Chapter 82

New Hampshire

Corporation Division Department of State
107 North Main Street
Concord, NH 03301
603-271-3244

Website:
www.sos.nh.gov/corporate

LIMITED LIABILITY COMPANY

WHAT MUST BE FILED:

The Certificate of Formation must be filed in duplicate and signed by a member or manager with his or her capacity designated. It must be accompanied by form LCC 1-A, Addendum to Certificate of Formation.

ARTICLES OF ORGANIZATION SPECIAL REQUIREMENTS:

The Certificate of Formation must list the nature of the primary business, but you may add the authority "to perform any lawful business permitted for limited liability companies under the state law." In New Hampshire, your LLC must certify in a separate addendum (Form LLC 1-A) that it meets the requirements of the New Hampshire Securities Law. If the aggregate number of holders of the company's securities does not exceed ten, provides that no advertising has been published in connection with any security sale, and all securities sales are consummated within sixty days after the date of the formation of the company, then the company is exempt from securities registration. If your company meets these requirements, check line 1 in the Addendum. If your company has or will register its securities for sale in New Hampshire, enter the date the registration statement was or will be filed with the Bureau of Securities Regulation in line 2. If you can take advantage of another exemption from the registration requirement, cite this exemption in line 3.

STATUTES:

New Hampshire Revised Statutes Annotated, beginning with Section 304-C:1.

CORPORATION

WHAT MUST BE FILED:

Print or type your documents in black ink and leave one-inch margins on both sides.

File the original and one exact copy. Both documents must bear original signatures. Note that your Articles of Agreement must be filed with the clerk of the city or town of the principal place of business prior to filing with the Secretary of State. Enclose the filing fee.

ARTICLES REQUIREMENTS:

The most important requirement for forming your nonprofit corporation is that you need five or more incorporators.

The legal purposes your corporation may be formed for are listed in Chapter 292:1 of the New Hampshire Revised Statutes.

In Article 7 you have the opportunity to make provisions eliminating or limiting the personal liability of a director or officer of your corporation.

STATUTE:

New Hampshire Revised Statutes Annotated Chapter 292

New Jersey

New Jersey Division of Revenue
Corporate Filing Unit
P.O. Box 628
Trenton, NJ 08646
609-292-9292

Website:
www.state.nj.us/njbgs/index.html

LIMITED LIABILITY COMPANY

WHAT MUST BE FILED:

You need to file the "Public Records Filing for New Business Entity" form and the "Business Registration" form. Those forms are for any new business, so make sure to check that you are forming a limited liability company.

To take part in the fax-filing program which offers same or next day filing, complete the "Facsimile Filing Service Request" and fax this request together with your completed Certificate of Formation to 609-984-6851. Payment method for this program is either by Visa/MC or Discover, or you have to give your depository account number. Note that there is an extra filing fee for the fax service (see "Filing Fees").

ARTICLES OF ORGANIZATION SPECIAL REQUIREMENTS:

You need to put in a type code in No. 2. The type code for your limited liability company is "LLC" (for a foreign: "FLC").

STATUTES:

New Jersey Revised Statutes Title 42:2B.

CORPORATION

WHAT MUST BE FILED:

Type your documents in black ink. File the original and two exact copies. Enclose a self-addressed stamped envelope to receive a filed copy and the correct filing fee.

ARTICLES REQUIREMENTS:

To obtain the tax exempt status after filing your Articles make sure the purpose for which your corporation is organized (Article 2) will meet the IRS requirements for tax exemption.

You can leave most of the regulation for the corporations inner affairs to your bylaws if you do not want these affairs to be regulated by the Certificate of Incorporation.

STATUTE:

New Jersey Statutes Sec. 15A:2-8

New Mexico

Public Regulation Commission
P.O. Box 1269
Santa Fe, NM 87504
505-827-4502
505-827-4508
800-947-4722
    (New Mexico residents only)

Website:
www.nmprc.state.nm.us/corporations/
    corpshome.htm

LIMITED LIABILITY COMPANY

WHAT MUST BE FILED:

An original and duplicate of Articles of Organization together with the notarized affidavit of the person appointed as your registered agent. Enclose the appropriate filing fee.

The filing office also accepts faxed filing documents.

ARTICLES OF ORGANIZATION SPECIAL REQUIREMENTS:

A notarized affidavit accepting appointment must be provided by the registered agent.

STATUTES:

New Mexico Statutes Annotated Title 53, Chapter 19.

CORPORATION

WHAT MUST BE FILED:

Type or print your Articles legibly in black ink. File duplicate originals and attach the completed, signed and notarized affidavit of acceptance of your registered agent. Enclose the correct filing fee.

ARTICLES REQUIREMENTS:

The minimum requirements for forming the corporation are as follows:

- the name of the corporation
- the period of its duration, which may be perpetual
- a definition of the purpose for which the corporation is formed
- provisions regulating the internal affairs of the corporation including provisions for distributing remaining assets upon the dissolution of the corporation
- the name of its initial agent and the address of the agent's office
- the number of persons serving as the initial directors and the names and addresses of these directors
- the name and address of each incorporator

STATUTE:

New Mexico Statutes Annotated Chapter 53-8-31

New York

NYS Department of State
Division of Corporations
41 State Street
Albany, N.Y. 12231
518-473-2492

Website:
www.dos.state.ny.us/corp/corpwww.html

LIMITED LIABILITY COMPANY

WHAT MUST BE FILED:

An original and duplicate of Articles of Organization.

If you reserved a name prior to filing, enclose a copy of the certificate of name registration.

ARTICLES OF ORGANIZATION SPECIAL REQUIREMENTS:

The secretary of state should be designated as agent for service of process. The county of the principal office must be listed.

Notice of formation must be published in two publications of general circulation, once a week for six weeks.

STATUTES:

Chapter 34 of the Consolidated Law, New York Limited Liability Company Law.

CORPORATION

WHAT MUST BE FILED:

If you draft your own Articles of Incorporation (not using the forms) make sure that your documents contain a separate page which sets forth the title of the document being submitted and the name and address of the person to which the receipt for filing shall be mailed. Enclose the filing fee.

ARTICLES REQUIREMENTS:

The Certificate of Incorporation must set forth the following minimum:

- the name of the corporation
- a statement that the corporation is formed pursuant to subparagraph (a)(5) of Section 102 of the Not-For-Profit Corporation Law, the type of corporation it shall be under section 201 (Type A-D), and the purpose for which the corporation is formed
- the county where the corporate office is to be located
- the name and address of each director, if your corporation is an A, B, or C type corporation
- the duration of the corporation, if not perpetual
- a designation of the Secretary of State as agent of the corporation upon whom process may be served and the P.O. address to which the secretary of state shall mail a copy on any process against it served upon him or her
- if applicable, the name of the registered agent and the address of its initial registered office and a statement that he or she is the agent upon whom process against the corporation may be served
- any provision for the regulation of the internal affairs of the corporation that is not inconsistent with the law (e.g., types or classes of membership, distribution of assets upon dissolution, etc.)

STATUTE:

New York Not-For-Profit Corporation Law, Sec. 402

North Carolina

Corporations Division
P.O. Box 29622
Raleigh, NC 27626
919-807-2225

Website:
www.secretary.state.nc.us./corporations

LIMITED LIABILITY COMPANY

WHAT MUST BE FILED:

An original and duplicate of Articles of Organization.

ARTICLES OF ORGANIZATION SPECIAL REQUIREMENTS:

Name and address of each organizer is required.

STATUTES:

North Carolina General Statutes Title 57C.

CORPORATION

WHAT MUST BE FILED:

Draft your Articles accordingly to the sample and the instructions given in the booklet. File the original and one exact copy together with the filing fee.

After filing the copy will be returned "file-stamped" to the incorporator(s).

ARTICLES REQUIREMENTS:

The Articles of Incorporation require the following minimum:

- the corporate name
- a statement, whether the corporation shall be a "charitable or religious corporation" pursuant to the North Carolina. General Statutes Sec. 55A-2-02 (a)(2)
- the name of the initial registered agent and the street address of its initial registered office (if mailing address is different, give the mailing address)
- the name and address of each incorporator (at least one incorporator required)
- a statement whether the corporation shall have members
- provisions regarding the distribution of assets upon the dissolution of the corporation
- the street address (and, if different, the mailing address) and county of the principal office
- the signature and capacity of each incorporator

STATUTE:

North Carolina General Statutes, Chapter 55A

North Dakota

Secretary of State
600 East Boulevard Avenue
Department 108
Bismarck, ND 58505
701-328-4284
or 800-352-0867 ext. 8-4284

Website:
www.state.nd.us/sec/businessserv

LIMITED LIABILITY COMPANY

WHAT MUST BE FILED:

An original and duplicate of Articles of Organization and a Registered Agent Consent to Serve.

ARTICLES OF ORGANIZATION SPECIAL REQUIREMENTS:

Must include name and address of each organizer.

STATUTES:

North Dakota Century Code. Chapter 10-32.

CORPORATION

WHAT MUST BE FILED:

Complete the Articles and file in duplicate. Attach the signed consent to serve and enclose the filing fee for the Articles and for the consent.

ARTICLES REQUIREMENTS:

The Articles require the following minimum:

- the name of the corporation
- if not perpetual, the duration of its existence
- a specific characterization of the purpose for which the corporation is formed
- provisions for the distribution of assets upon the dissolution or final liquidation of the corporation
- the name of the initial registered agent and the address of the agent's registered office
- the number of your initial directors and their names and addresses

STATUTE:

North Dakota Century Code Chapter 10-33

Ohio

Secretary of State
Corporations Division
180 East Broad Street
Columbus, OH 43215
614-466-3910
877-767-3453

Website:
www.sos.state.oh.us/sos/
   busiserv/index.html

LIMITED LIABILITY COMPANY

WHAT MUST BE FILED:

One copy of each of Articles of Organization and Original Appointment of Agent. The Appointment must be signed by a majority of members and by the agent.

ARTICLES OF ORGANIZATION SPECIAL REQUIREMENTS:

The Articles must be accompanied by an Original Appointment of Agent signed by a majority of members and by the agent.

STATUTES:

Title 17, Chapter 1705 of the Ohio Revised Code, Limited Liability Companies.

CORPORATION

WHAT MUST BE FILED:

Complete the fill-in-the-blanks Articles and file them with the Secretary of State. Make sure that the Articles are signed by the incorporators and their names are printed or typed beneath their signatures. Enclose the filing fee. The trustees do not have to sign the Articles.

ARTICLES REQUIREMENTS:

The basic requirements are as follows:

- the corporate name
- the names and addresses of the initial trustees (not fewer than three natural persons)
- name and address of a statutory agent
- the specific purpose of the corporation (a general purpose clause will not be accepted)

STATUTE:

Ohio Revised Code, Chapter 1702.04

Oklahoma

Secretary of State
Business Filing Department
2300 North Lincoln Boulevard
Room 101
101 State Capitol Building
Oklahoma City, OK 73105
405-521-3912

Website:
www.sos.state.ok.us/business/
   business_filing.htm

LIMITED LIABILITY COMPANY

WHAT MUST BE FILED:

Two copies of the Articles must be filed.

ARTICLES OF ORGANIZATION SPECIAL REQUIREMENTS:

No unusual requirements.

STATUTES:

Title 18, Chapter 32 of the Oklahoma Statutes, Oklahoma Limited Liability Company Act.

CORPORATION

WHAT MUST BE FILED:

Type or print your documents clearly and file the original in duplicate. Enclose the filing fee.

ARTICLES REQUIREMENTS:

The basic requirements are as follows:

- the corporate name
- the name of the initial registered agent and the address of its initial registered office
- if the corporation is a church, the street address of its location
- if not perpetual, the duration of your corporation
- the specific purpose for which the corporation is formed
- the number, names, and mailing addresses of the initial directors
- the names and mailing address of each incorporator

Make sure that each incorporator signs the Articles.

STATUTE:

Oklahoma Statutes, Title 18, Oklahoma General Corporation Act

Oregon

State of Oregon
Corporation Division
255 Capitol Street NE
Suite 151
Salem, OR 97310
503-986-2200
Fax: 503-378-4381

Website:
www.filinginoregon.com

LIMITED LIABILITY COMPANY

WHAT MUST BE FILED:

Original and one copy.

ARTICLES OF ORGANIZATION SPECIAL REQUIREMENTS:

Name and address of each organizer must be included.

STATUTES:

Title 7, Chapter 63 Oregon Revised Statutes, Oregon Limited Liability Company Act.

CORPORATION

WHAT MUST BE FILED:

Type or print the Articles in black ink. If you file your documents by mail, attach one exact copy of the original. Enclose the filing fee.

ARTICLES REQUIREMENTS:

The basic requirements are as follows:

- corporate name
- name and address of registered agent (the address must be an Oregon street address and identical with the agent's business office, post office boxes are not acceptable)
- the agent's mailing address
- corporation's address for mailing notices
- type of corporation (public benefit, mutual benefit, religious)
- a statement whether the corporation will have members or not
- a statement concerning the distribution of assets upon dissolution
- names and addresses of all incorporators

Make sure that each incorporator signs the document and print or typewrite the names beneath the signatures.

STATUTE:

Oregon Revised Statutes, Chapter 65 Oregon Business Corporation Act

Pennsylvania

Department of State
Corporation Bureau
206 North Office Building
Harrisburg, PA 17120
717-787-1057

Website:
www.dos.state.pa.us/corps/site/default.asp

LIMITED LIABILITY COMPANY

WHAT MUST BE FILED:

One original Certificate of Organization–Domestic Limited Liability Company and one copy of the completed docketing statement (form DSCB:15-134A).

Also include either a self-addressed, stamped postcard with the filing information noted or a self-addressed, stamped envelope with a copy of the filing document to receive confirmation of the file date prior to receiving the microfilmed original.

ARTICLES OF ORGANIZATION SPECIAL REQUIREMENTS:

Must list names and addresses of all members and organizers.

STATUTES:

Title 15, Chapter 89, Pennsylvania Consolidated Statutes.

CORPORATION

WHAT MUST BE FILED:

Print or type your documents in black or blue-black ink. File the original of your Articles of Incorporation, attach a cover letter and enclose the following:

- one copy of the completed docketing statement (form DSCB: 15-134A)—this form is provided by the state
- if applicable, copies of the Consent to Appropriation of Name or, copies of the Consent to Use of Similar Name
- the filing fee

Also include either a self-addressed, stamped postcard with the filing information noted or a self-addressed, stamped envelope with a copy of the filing document to receive confirmation of the file date prior to receiving the microfilmed original.

ARTICLES REQUIREMENTS:

If you want to apply for the federal tax exemption, check with the IRS prior to filing your Articles to make sure your corporation meets the special purpose required to qualify for the tax exemption (purpose must be given in Article 3).

Give the name and address of each incorporator in Article 8 (minimum of one incorporator).

STATUTE:

Pennsylvania Consolidated Statutes Title 15

Rhode Island

Secretary of State
Corporations Division
100 North Main Street
Providence, RI 02903
401-222-3040

Website:
www.sec.state.ri.us/us/corps

LIMITED LIABILITY COMPANY

WHAT MUST BE FILED:

Two signed copies of the Articles of Organization must be filed.

ARTICLES OF ORGANIZATION SPECIAL REQUIREMENTS:

A statement should be included indicating whether the company is to be taxed as a corporation or pass-through entity.

STATUTES:

Title 7, Chapter 16 of the General Laws of Rhode Island.

CORPORATION

WHAT MUST BE FILED:

Complete and sign the original and the duplicate Articles. Enclose the filing fee.

When the Articles are properly completed, a Certificate of Incorporation, together with the file stamped original will be returned to you.

ARTICLES REQUIREMENTS:

The minimum requirements are as follows:

- the corporate name
- if not perpetual, the duration of the corporation
- the specific purpose your corporation is formed for (if you want to apply for the federal tax exemption, check with the IRS prior to filing if your corporation must meet specific requirements)
- any provisions for regulating the corporation's internal affairs
- the name of the initial registered agent and the address of its initial registered office
- the number of directors and their names and addresses
- the name and address of each incorporator

Make sure that each incorporator signs the Articles.

STATUTE:

General Laws Rhode Island Chapter 7-6-34

South Carolina

Secretary of State
P.O. Box 11350
Columbia, SC 29211
803-734-2158

Website:
www.scsos.com/corporations.htm

LIMITED LIABILITY COMPANY

WHAT MUST BE FILED:

File the completed original and one copy (duplicate, original, or conformed copy). Enclose the
filing fee.

ARTICLES OF ORGANIZATION SPECIAL
REQUIREMENTS:

On the Articles of Organization form provided
by the state, article 7 allows the company to
designate one or more of its members to be
liable for company debts. This is neither
required nor recommended and defeats the
purpose of the limited liability company.

STATUTES:

Chapter 33-44 of the South Carolina Code of
1976.

CORPORATION

WHAT MUST BE FILED:

File the completed original and either a duplicate original or a conformed copy. Enclose the
filing fee.

ARTICLES REQUIREMENTS:

In Article 3 check the appropriate box whether
the corporation is a public benefit, religious, or
mutual benefit corporation. If you want to apply
for the federal tax exemption and your corporation is either a public benefit or religious corporation, check the "a" box in Article 6 to make
sure that upon dissolution of the corporation,
the assets will be distributed accordingly to the
tax exempt purposes. If you form a mutual
benefit corporation check one of the two dissolution statements in Article 7.

Each incorporator (minimum of one) must sign
the Articles.

STATUTE:

South Carolina Code Annotated Chapter 33-44

South Dakota

Secretary of State
Capitol Building
500 East Capital Avenue
Suite 204
Pierre, SD 57501
605-773-4845

Website:
www.sdsos.gov/corporations

LIMITED LIABILITY COMPANY

WHAT MUST BE FILED:

Two copies of the Articles of Organization and a First Annual Report.

ARTICLES OF ORGANIZATION SPECIAL REQUIREMENTS:

The duration of the LLC can be for no more than thirty years (though it can be extended in the future). Total cash, property, and services contributed must be listed as well as requirements for future contributions.

If there are managers, their names and residence addresses must be included; otherwise, the name and residence addresses of the members must be listed.

On the Articles of Organization form provided by the state, Article 7 allows the company to designate one or more of its members to be liable for company debts. This is neither required nor recommended and defeats the purpose of the limited liability company.

A first Annual Report must be filed along with the Articles.

STATUTES:

South Dakota Codified Laws, Title 47, Chapters 34 and 34A.

CORPORATION

WHAT MUST BE FILED:

Type the Articles and file the original document and one exact copy. Make sure that the consent of appointment is signed by the registered agent and that the Articles are notarized. Enclose the filing fee.

ARTICLES REQUIREMENTS:

The Articles must contain the following minimum:

- the name of the corporation
- if not perpetual, the period of existence
- the purpose for which the corporation is formed—this clause must contain sufficient information to determine the type of purpose (types of purposes are given in Section 47-22-4 of the statutes)
- a statement whether the corporation shall have members and if so, provisions regulating the class of members and their rights
- regulations concerning the method of election of the directors
- any provisions regulating the internal affairs of the corporation
- the street address of your initial registered office and the name or your initial registered agent
- the number of directors and their names and addresses
- the names and addresses of the incorporators (minimum of three)
- the signature of each incorporator

STATUTE:

South Dakota Codified Laws Chapter 47

Tennessee

Department of State
Corporate Filings
312 Eighth Avenue North
6th Floor
William R. Snodgrass Tower
Nashville, TN 37243
615-741-2286

Website:
www.tennessee.gov/sos/bus_svc/index.htm

LIMITED LIABILITY COMPANY

WHAT MUST BE FILED:

Only one original Articles of Organization must be filed.

ARTICLES OF ORGANIZATION SPECIAL REQUIREMENTS:

The name and address of each organizer must be listed. The county and zip code of the registered office and the principle executive office must be included with their addresses. The number of members must be listed.

If a member can be expelled and if there are prescriptive rights, these must be spelled out in the Articles. It is possible to designate one or more of its members to be liable for company debts. This is neither required nor recommended, as it defeats the purpose of the limited liability company.

STATUTES:

Tennessee Code Annotated, Sections 48-201-101 through 48-248-606.

CORPORATION

WHAT MUST BE FILED:

Type or print the Articles in black ink using either the fill-in-the-blanks form or, if drafting your own documents, using legal or letter size paper. The documents must be executed either by an incorporator, by the chair of the board of directors, or by a trustee. File only the original document(s) together with the filing fee.

ARTICLES REQUIREMENTS:

The charter must contain the following minimum:

- the corporate name
- a statement whether the corporation is a public or mutual benefit corporation or whether it is a religious corporation
- the address of the initial registered office and the name of the initial registered agent
- the name and address of each incorporator
- the street address of the principal office (may be the same as the address of the registered agent)
- a statement that the corporation is not for profit
- a statement that there will be no members
- provisions regarding the distribution of assets upon the dissolution of the corporation

STATUTE:

Tennessee Code Annotated Section 48-52

Texas

Corporations Section
Office of the Secretary of State
P.O. Box 13697
Austin, TX 78711
512-463-5555

Website:
www.sos.state.tx.us/corp/index.shtml

LIMITED LIABILITY COMPANY

WHAT MUST BE FILED:

Two copies of the Articles must be filed. Use the P. O. Box for mail. For courier use: James Earl Rudder, Office Building, 1019 Brazos, Austin, TX 78701.

ARTICLES OF ORGANIZATION SPECIAL REQUIREMENTS:

The name and address of each organizer must be included.

STATUTES:

Texas Rev. Civil Statutes Annotated Art. 1528n, Texas Limited Liability Company Act.

CORPORATION

WHAT MUST BE FILED:

Draft your own Articles accordingly to the instructions provided by the state or fill out the form provided. File two copies of these together with the filing fee. The filing office will return one filed stamped copy.

ARTICLES REQUIREMENTS:

The minimum contents of your Articles are as follows:

- the name of the corporation
- the period of duration, which may be perpetual
- a statement that the corporation is not for profit
- the specific purpose for which the corporation is formed (check with the IRS prior to filing what requirements your corporation has to meet to qualify for the federal tax exemption)
- the name of the registered agent and the address of the registered office.
- a statement whether the corporation shall have members
- if the management of the corporation shall be vested in the members, a statement to that effect
- the number of the initial board of directors and the names and addresses of your directors
- the name and street address of each incorporator
- provisions regarding the distribution of assets upon the dissolution of the corporation

Make sure that each incorporator signs the Articles.

STATUTE:

Texas Nonprofit Corporation Act, Article 1396-3.02

Utah

Department of Commerce
Division of Corporations and
    Commercial Code
P.O. Box 146705
Salt Lake City, UT 84114
801-530-4849
877-526-3994 (in state)

Website:
www.commerce.utah.gov/cor/index.html

LIMITED LIABILITY COMPANY

WHAT MUST BE FILED:

File one original and one exact copy of your
Articles. You can deliver the documents personally, by mail or by fax. If you choose to fax your
documents, make sure to include the number of
your Visa/MasterCard and the expiration date.

ARTICLES OF ORGANIZATION SPECIAL
REQUIREMENTS:

The period of duration cannot exceed ninety-
nine years. If there are managers, their names
and residence addresses must be included,
otherwise the name and residence addresses of
the members must be listed.

STATUTES:

Utah Code Annotated, Title 48-2B.

CORPORATION

WHAT MUST BE FILED:

File one original and one exact copy of your self-
drafted Articles. At least one document must
bear the original signature. You can deliver the
documents personally, by mail, or even by fax. If
you choose to fax your documents, make sure to
include the number of your Visa/Mastercard
and the expiration date.

ARTICLES REQUIREMENTS:

The minimum of what the Articles must
contain is:

- the corporate name
- the term of the corporation's existence
- the purpose or purposes for which your
  corporation is formed—this must include
  the statement that it is organized as a
  nonprofit corporation
- the address of the corporation's principal
  office
- a statement whether or not the corporation shall have members
- the number of initial trustees your
  corporation shall have and their names
  and addresses
- the name and street address of each
  incorporator (at least one)
- the name of the corporation's initial
  registered agent and the street address of
  the registered office
- the signature of each incorporator

The Articles also must include a statement by
your registered agent that he or she acknowl-
edges his or her acceptance as registered agent.

STATUTE:

Utah Code Annotated, Section 16-6-46
Corporation Laws

Vermont

Secretary of State
81 River Street
Montpelier, VT 05609
802-828-2386

Website:
www.sec.state.vt.us/corps/corpindex.htm

LIMITED LIABILITY COMPANY

WHAT MUST BE FILED:

The original and one exact copy.

ARTICLES OF ORGANIZATION SPECIAL REQUIREMENTS:

The name and address of each organizer are required.

It is possible to designate one or more of the company's members to be liable for company debts. This is neither required nor recommended, as it defeats the purpose of the limited liability company. However, you need to include a statement about it in your Articles.

STATUTES:

Vermont Statutes Annotated, Title 11, Chapter 21, beginning with Section 3001.

CORPORATION

WHAT MUST BE FILED:

Complete the fill-in-the-blanks form by typewriting or printing. File the original and one exact copy. Enclose the filing fee.

ARTICLES REQUIREMENTS:

The minimum requirements are as follows:

- the corporate name
- the name of the registered agent
- the street address of the registered office
- if not perpetual, the period of duration
- a statement, whether the corporation shall be a public benefit, mutual benefit, nonprofit corporation, or a cooperative
- the names and addresses of your initial directors
- if applicable, the names and addresses of your members
- the specific purpose for which your corporation is formed
- provisions regarding the distribution of assets upon the dissolution of the corporation
- signatures and addresses of each incorporator

STATUTE:

Vermont Statutes Annotated, Title 11, Nonprofit Corporations

Virginia

Clerk of the State
   Corporation Commission
P.O. Box 1197
Richmond, VA 23218
804-371-9733

Website:
www.state.va.us/scc/division/clk

LIMITED LIABILITY COMPANY

WHAT MUST BE FILED:

The Articles must be printed or typewritten in black ink. Complete and file the original form and enclose the filing fee.

ARTICLES OF ORGANIZATION SPECIAL REQUIREMENTS:

The registered agent must be an individual who is a Virginia resident and either a member or an officer, director or partner of a member of the LLC, or a Virginia State Bar member, or an organization registered under Va. Code Section 54.1-3902 (an attorney's PC, PLLC, or PRLLP) and this must be stated in the Articles.

The city or county of the registered agent must be included and also the post office address of the office where the records will be kept.

The Articles can be executed by any person.

STATUTES:

Title 13.1 of the Code of Virginia.

CORPORATION

WHAT MUST BE FILED:

For forming a nonprofit corporation take form SCC 819 (nonstock corporation). Type or write your Articles in black ink. Complete and file only the original form and enclose the filing fee.

ARTICLES REQUIREMENTS:

The minimum requirements for filing the Articles are as follows:

- the corporate name
- a statement whether or not your corporation shall have members and if so, provisions designating the classes of members and their rights
- a statement of the manner in which directors shall be elected or appointed
- the name of the initial registered agent and its status
- the address of your registered office
- optional provisions regarding the purpose for which the corporation is formed (to meet the special requirements for obtaining the federal tax exempt status, check with the IRS prior to filing the Articles for which requirements have to be met)
- if the corporation shall have initial directors, state the number of directors and their names and addresses
- the signature and printed name of each incorporator

STATUTE:

Virginia Code Annotated Title 13.1 Chapter 10

Washington

Secretary of State
Corporations Division
P.O. Box 40234
Olympia, WA 98504
360-753-7115

Website:
www.secstate.wa.gov/corps

LIMITED LIABILITY COMPANY

WHAT MUST BE FILED:

Type or print the document in black ink. Submit original and one copy. If expedited service is desired write "expedited" in bold letters on outside of envelope and include the additional fee.

ARTICLES OF ORGANIZATION SPECIAL REQUIREMENTS:

There are no unusual requirements.

STATUTES:

Chapter 25.15 Revised Code of Washington.

CORPORATION

WHAT MUST BE FILED:

Type or print the document in black ink. Submit the original and one copy together with the filing fee. An expedited service (filing within 24 hours) is available for an extra $20 fee. If you want the expedited service write "expedited" in bold letters on outside of envelope.

ARTICLES REQUIREMENTS:

At a minimum, the Articles must contain the following:

- the name of the corporation
- if wanted, a specific effective date of incorporation
- the term of existence
- the purpose for which the corporation is formed
- provisions regulating the distribution of assets upon dissolution of the corporation
- the name and street address of the initial registered agent and a signature by this agent, acknowledging acceptance
- the name and address of each initial director
- the name and address of each incorporator
- the signature of each incorporator

STATUTE:

Washington Revised Code Chapter 24.03

West Virginia

Secretary of State
Building 1, Suite 157-K
1900 Kanawha Boulevard East
Charleston, WV 25305
304-558-8000

Website:
www.wvsos.com/business/main.htm

LIMITED LIABILITY COMPANY

WHAT MUST BE FILED:

Two original copies of the Articles of Organization must be filed.

ARTICLES OF ORGANIZATION SPECIAL REQUIREMENTS:

It is possible to designate members to be liable for company debts. This is neither required nor recommended, as it defeats the purpose of the limited liability company. However, the statement needs to be included in your Articles.

STATUTES:

Chapter 31B, beginning with Section 1-101, Uniform Limited Liability Company Act.

CORPORATION

WHAT MUST BE FILED:

Complete the Articles and file both originals. Make sure that the incorporator(s) file both documents and that the documents are notarized. Enclose the filing fee.

ARTICLES REQUIREMENTS:

The fill-in-the-blanks form provided by the State is both for stock and non-stock (nonprofit) corporations. Check the "nonprofit" box in Article 5 to denote your corporation structure. Then state the purpose your corporation is formed for in Article 7 and check the appropriate box whether provisions regulating the internal affairs of the corporation shall be set forth in the bylaws or are attached to the Articles. Give the names and street addresses of the incorporators in Article 10 and the names and number of initial directors in Article 11.

Name at least one person who shall have signature authority on documents filed with the Secretary of State (annual report). The incorporators must sign the Articles. Make sure that the signatures are notarized.

STATUTE:

West Virginia Code Section 31-1-27

Wisconsin

Department of Financial Institutions
Division of Corporate and
  Consumer Services
P.O. Box 7846
Madison, WI 53707
608-261-7577

Website:
www.wisconsin.gov or
www.wdfi.org/corporations

LIMITED LIABILITY COMPANY

WHAT MUST BE FILED:

Original and one copy must be filed.

For expedited service (filing procedure will be complete the next business day), mark your documents "For Expedited Service" and provide an extra $25 for each item. Indicate on the back side of your Articles where you would like the acknowledgement copy of the filed document sent.

Use the above address for mail. For courier delivery use 345 West Washington Avenue, 3rd Floor, Madison, WI 53703.

ARTICLES SPECIAL OF ORGANIZATION REQUIREMENTS:

The Articles for a Wisconsin LLC can only contain items of information such as:

- The name
- The street address of the initial registered office
- The name of the initial registered agent at the above address
- Whether management is vested in the members or manager(s)
- The name, address, and signature of each organizer
- A statement that the company is organized under Wisconsin statutes, Chapter 183
- The name of the person who drafted the articles

Other terms between members can be included in the operating agreement.

STATUTES:

Chapter 183 of the Wisconsin Statutes.

CORPORATION

WHAT MUST BE FILED:

Complete the fill-in-the-blanks forms and send the original and one copy to the Department of Financial Institutions. Enclose the filing fee. For expedited service (filing procedure will be completed the next business day), mark your documents "For Expedited Service" and provide an extra $25 for each item. Indicate on the back side of your Articles where the acknowledgement copy of the filed document should be sent.

ARTICLES REQUIREMENTS:

The minimum requirements are as follows:

- corporate name
- the phrase: "The corporation is organized under Chapter 181 of the Wisconsin Statutes"
- name and address of the registered agent (street address of the agent's office is required, post office box address may be part of the address, but is sufficient alone)
- mailing address of the corporation's principal office (it may be located outside of Wisconsin)
- a statement whether the corporation will have members or not
- name, address, and signature of each incorporator
- name of the person who drafted the document (printed, typewritten or stamped in a legible manner)

STATUTE:

Wisconsin Statutes, Chapter 181

Wyoming

Corporations Division
Secretary of State
The Capital Building
Room 110
200 West 24th Street
Cheyenne, WY 82002
307-777-7311

Website:
http://soswy.state.wy.us/corporat/
corporat.htm

LIMITED LIABILITY COMPANY

WHAT MUST BE FILED:

An original and one exact copy must be filed along with a written consent to appointment by the registered agent.

ARTICLES OF ORGANIZATION SPECIAL REQUIREMENTS:

The total of cash, a description, the agreed value of property other than cash contributed to the company, and any additional capital agreed to be contributed must be included in the Articles.

If there is a right to admit new members the terms of admission must be stated.

If the members have a right to continue the business after the termination of a member this must be stated.

The Articles must accompany a written consent by the registered agent to appointment as agent.

STATUTES:

Wyoming Statute beginning with 17-15-101.

CORPORATION

WHAT MUST BE FILED:

Complete the forms and file the original and one exact copy. The Articles must be accompanied by the written consent to appointment executed by the registered agent. Enclose the filing fee.

ARTICLES REQUIREMENTS:

The Articles must contain the following minimum:

- the corporate name
- a statement whether the corporation is a religious, a public benefit or a mutual benefit corporation
- the street address of your corporation's initial registered office and the name of the registered agent
- the name and address of each incorporator
- a statement whether your corporation shall have members
- provisions regarding the distribution of assets upon the dissolution of the corporation
- the date and signature of each incorporator

Do not forget to let your registered agent sign the "Consent to Appointment."

STATUTE:

Wyoming Statute, Section 17-6-102

Appendix

Blank Forms

This appendix contains blank operating agreements for both management and membership operating agreements for a limited liability company, which you can adapt for your own LLC. Also included is a form to make amendments to your operating agreement. You will also find a sample shareholder agreement, if you are forming a corporation instead. (Be sure to check with your state to see if it has any specific forms you should use instead.)

When photocopying, be sure to expand the page to 8.5"x11" so the documents will be accepted in court and by government agencies.

TABLE OF FORMS

Limited Liability Company Management Operating Agreement of
_____, LLC

THIS AGREEMENT is made effective as of _____, 2006 between the members and the company.

1. Formation. A limited liability company of the above name has been formed under the laws of the state of _____ by filing articles of organization with the secretary of state. The purpose of the business shall be to carry on any act or activity lawful under the jurisdiction in which it operates. The company may operate under a fictitious name or names as long as the company is in compliance with applicable fictitious name registration laws. The term of the company shall be perpetual or until dissolved as provided by law or by vote of the members as provided in this agreement. Upon dissolution the remaining members shall have the power to continue the operation of the company as long as necessary and allowable under state law until the winding up of the affairs of the business has been completed.

2. Members. The initial members shall be listed on Schedule A, which shall accompany and be made a part of this agreement. Additional members may be admitted to membership upon the unanimous consent of the current members. Transfer or pledge of a member's interest may not be made except upon consent of all members.

3. Contributions. The initial capital contributions shall be listed on Schedule A, which shall accompany and be made a part of this agreement. No member shall be obligated to contribute any more than the amount set forth on Schedule A unless agreed to in writing by all of the members and managers and no member shall have any personal liability for any debt, obligation or liability of the company other than for full payment of his or her capital contribution. No member shall be entitled to interest on the capital contribution. Member voting rights shall be in proportion to the amount of their contributions.

4. Business Purpose. The company has been organized for the business purpose of _____.

5. Profit and Loss. The profits and losses of the business, and all other taxable or deductible items shall be allocated to the members according to the percentages on Schedule A, which shall accompany and be made a part of this agreement.

6. Distributions. The company shall have the power to make distributions to its members in such amounts and at such intervals as a majority of the members deem appropriate according to law.

7. Management. The limited liability company shall be managed by the managers listed on Schedule A, which shall accompany and be made a part of this agreement. These managers may or may not be members of the company and each manager shall have an equal vote with other managers as to management decisions. Managers shall serve until resignation or death or until they are removed by a majority vote of the members. Replacement managers shall be selected by a majority vote of the members. Managers shall have no personal liability for expenses, obligations or liabilities of the company.

8. Fiduciary Duty. Each member of the company shall have a fiduciary duty to each other member and to the company to act in the best interests of the company in all dealing with and for the company.

9. Registered Agent. The company shall at all times have a registered agent and registered office. The initial registered agent and registered office shall be listed on Schedule A, which shall accompany and be made a part of this agreement.

10. Assets. The assets of the company shall be registered in the legal name of the company and not in the names of the individual members.

11. Records and Accounting. The company shall keep an accurate accounting of its affairs using any method of accounting allowed by law. All members shall have a right to inspect the records during normal business hours. The members shall have the power to hire such accountants as they deem necessary or desirable.

12. Banking. The members of the company shall be authorized to set up bank accounts as in their sole discretion are deemed necessary and are authorized to execute any banking resolutions provided by the institution in which the accounts are being set up.

13. Taxes. The company shall file such tax returns as required by law. The company shall elect to be taxed as a majority of the members decide is in their best interests. The "tax matters partner," as required by the Internal Revenue Code, shall be listed on Schedule A, which shall accompany and be made a part of this agreement.

14. Separate Entity. The company is a legal entity separate from its members. No member shall have any separate liability for any debts, obligations or liability of the company except as provided in this agreement.

15. Indemnity and Exculpation. The limited liability company shall indemnify and hold harmless its members, managers, employees and agents to the fullest extent allowed by law for acts or omissions done as part of their duties to or for the company. Indemnification shall include all liabilities, expenses, attorney and accountant fees, and other costs reasonably expended. No member shall be liable to the company for acts done in good faith.

16. Meetings. The company shall have no obligation to hold annual or any other meeting, but may hold such meetings if deemed necessary or desirable. However, each member shall participate in the management and decisions of the company. When meetings are held, each member of the company shall attend. No member shall be required to take any action which would result in personal liability for that member.

17. Executive Contract. The parties desire that this agreement shall constitute an executive contract under 1 U.S.C. §365.

18. Amendment of this Agreement. This agreement may not be amended except in writing signed by all of the members.

19. Conflict of Interest. No member shall be involved with any business or undertaking which competes with the interests of the company except upon agreement in writing by all of the members.

20. Deadlock. In the event that the members cannot come to an agreement on any matter the members agree to submit the issue to mediation to be paid for by the company. In the event the mediation is unsuccessful, they agree to seek arbitration under the rules of the American Arbitration Association.

21. Dissociation of a Member. A member shall have the right to discontinue membership upon giving thirty days notice. A member shall cease to have the right to membership upon death, court-ordered incapacity, bankruptcy or expulsion. The company shall have the right to buy the interest of any dissociated member at fair market value.

22. Dissolution. The company shall dissolve upon the unanimous consent of all the members or upon any event requiring dissolution under state law. In the event of the death, bankruptcy, permanent incapacity, or withdrawal of a member the remaining members may elect to dissolve or to continue the continuation of the company.

23. General Provisions. This agreement is intended to represent the entire agreement between the parties. In the event that any party of this agreement is held to be contrary to law or unenforceable, said party shall be considered amended to comply with the law and such holding shall not affect the enforceability of other terms of this agreement. This agreement shall be binding upon the heirs, successors and assigns of the members.

24. Miscellaneous. _____
_____
_____
_____
_____
_____

IN WITNESS whereof, the members of the limited liability company sign this agreement and adopt it as their operating agreement.

_____   _____

_____   _____

The undersigned accepts the position of manager and all of the responsibilities and duties thereof.

_____
_____, Manager

Limited Liability Company Member-Managed Operating Agreement of
_____, LLC

THIS AGREEMENT is made effective as of _____, 2007 between the members and the company.

1. Formation. A limited liability company of the above name has been formed under the laws of the state of _____ by filing articles of organization with the secretary of state. The purpose of the business shall be to carry on any act or activity lawful under the jurisdiction in which it operates. The company may operate under a fictitious name or names as long as the company is in compliance with applicable fictitious name registration laws. The term of the company shall be perpetual or until dissolved as provided by law or by vote of the members as provided in this agreement. Upon dissolution the remaining members shall have the power to continue the operation of the company as long as necessary and allowable under state law until the winding up of the affairs of the business has been completed.

2. Members. The initial members shall be listed on Schedule A, which shall accompany and be made a part of this agreement. Additional members may be admitted to membership upon the unanimous consent of the current members. Transfer or pledge of a member's interest may not be made except upon consent of all members.

3. Contributions. The initial capital contributions shall be listed on Schedule A, which shall accompany and be made a part of this agreement. No member shall be obligated to contribute any more than the amount set forth on Schedule A unless agreed to in writing by all of the members and no member shall have any personal liability for any debt, obligation or liability of the company other than for full payment of his or her capital contribution. No member shall be entitled to interest on the capital contribution. Member voting rights shall be in proportion to the amount of their contributions.

4. Business Purpose. The company has been organized for the business purpose of _____
_____.

5. Profit and Loss. The profits and losses of the business, and all other taxable or deductible items shall be allocated to the members according to the percentages on Schedule A, which shall accompany and be made a part of this agreement.

6. Distributions. The company shall have the power to make distributions to its members in such amounts and at such intervals as a majority of the members deem appropriate according to law.

7. Management. The limited liability company shall be managed by its members listed on Schedule A. In the event of a dispute between members, final determination shall be made with a vote by the members, votes being proportioned according to capital contributions.

8. Fiduciary Duty. Each member of the company shall have a fiduciary duty to each other member and to the company to act in the best interests of the company in all dealing with and for the company.

9. Registered Agent. The company shall at all times have a registered agent and registered office. The initial registered agent and registered office shall be listed on Schedule A, which shall accompany and be made a part of this agreement.

10. Assets. The assets of the company shall be registered in the legal name of the company and not in the names of the individual members.

11. Records and Accounting. The company shall keep an accurate accounting of its affairs using any method of accounting allowed by law. All members shall have a right to inspect the records during normal business hours. The members shall have the power to hire such accountants as they deem necessary or desirable.

12. Banking. The members of the company shall be authorized to set up bank accounts as in their sole discretion are deemed necessary and are authorized to execute any banking resolutions provided by the institution in which the accounts are being set up.

13. Taxes. The company shall file such tax returns as required by law. The company shall elect to be taxed as a majority of the members decide is in their best interests. The "tax matters partner," as required by the Internal Revenue Code, shall be listed on Schedule A, which shall accompany and be made a part of this agreement.

14. Separate Entity. The company is a legal entity separate from its members. No member shall have any separate liability for any debts, obligations or liability of the company except as provided in this agreement.

15. Indemnity and Exculpation. The limited liability company shall indemnify and hold harmless its members, managers, employees and agents to the fullest extent allowed by law for acts or omissions done as part of their duties to or for the company. Indemnification shall include all liabilities, expenses, attorney and accountant fees, and other costs reasonably expended. No member shall be liable to the company for acts done in good faith.

16. Meetings. The company shall have no obligation to hold annual or any other meeting, but may hold such meetings if deemed necessary or desirable. However, each member shall participate in the management and decisions of the company. When meetings are held, each member of the company shall attend. No member shall be required to take any action which would result in personal liability for that member.

17. Executive Contract. The parties desire that this agreement shall constitute an executive contract under 1 U.S.C. §365.

18. Amendment of this Agreement. This agreement may not be amended except in writing signed by all of the members.

19. Conflict of Interest. No member shall be involved with any business or undertaking which competes with the interests of the company except upon agreement in writing by all of the members.

20. Deadlock. In the event that the members cannot come to an agreement on any matter the members agree to submit the issue to mediation to be paid for by the company. In the event the mediation is unsuccessful, they agree to seek arbitration under the rules of the American Arbitration Association.

21. Dissociation of a Member. A member shall have the right to discontinue membership upon giving thirty days notice. A member shall cease to have the right to membership upon death, court-ordered incapacity, bankruptcy or expulsion. The company shall have the right to buy the interest of any dissociated member at fair market value.

22. Dissolution. The company shall dissolve upon the unanimous consent of all the members or upon any event requiring dissolution under state law. In the event of the death, bankruptcy, permanent incapacity, or withdrawal of a member the remaining members may elect to dissolve or to continue the continuation of the company.

23. General Provisions. This agreement is intended to represent the entire agreement between the parties. In the event that any party of this agreement is held to be contrary to law or unenforceable, said party shall be considered amended to comply with the law and such holding shall not affect the enforceability of other terms of this agreement. This agreement shall be binding upon the heirs, successors and assigns of the members.

24. Miscellaneous. _____

_____

_____

_____

_____

_____

IN WITNESS whereof, the members of the limited liability company sign this agreement and adopt it as their operating agreement.

_____   _____

Amendment of Operating Agreement of

_____

a _____ Limited Liability Company

The undersigned, being all of the members and/or managers of the above-named Limited Liability Company hereby amend the company's Operating Agreement or Management Agreement as follows:

The following provisions (if checked) are added to the agreement:

☐ The parties agree that the LLC has been organized for the business purpose of _____

_____

☐ The parties desire that the Operating Agreement or Management Agreement as amended by this agreement shall constitute an executive contract under 1 U.S.C. §365.

☐ Each member of the company shall have an affirmative duty to provide additional capital to the company as decided by the management to be needed to the operation of the business.

☐ Each member of the company shall have a fiduciary duty to each other member and to the company to act in the best interests of the company in all dealing with and for the company.

☐ Each member of the company shall attend all regular and special meetings and to participate in the management of the company, provided however, that no member shall be required to take any action which would result in personal liability for that member.

Effective date: _____, 200___

_____

_____

_____

_____

SHAREHOLDER AGREEMENT

WHEREAS the undersigned shareholders are forming a Corporation and wish to protect their interests and those of the Corporation, in consideration of the mutual promises and conditions set out below, the parties agree as follows:

1. **Best Efforts.** Each shareholder agrees to devote his or her best efforts to the development of the Corporation. No shareholder shall participate in any enterprise which competes in any way with the activities of the Corporation.

2. **Right to Serve as Director or Officer.** Each shareholder shall, so long as he or she owns shares in the Corporation, have the right to serve as a director of the Corporation or to designate some responsible person to serve as his or her nominee.

The officers of the Corporation shall be the following shareholders, each of whom shall continue to serve as long as he owns shares:

President _____
Vice President _____
Treasurer _____
Secretary _____

Any officer or director who ceases to be a shareholder shall no longer be an officer or director upon the transfer of shares.

3. **Salary.** The Corporation shall employ the shareholders and pay salaries to them as follows:

Name of Shareholder and initial salary

_____ $_____
_____ $_____
_____ $_____

The salary received by any shareholder as an officer or employee or in any other function or for any other service shall serve as compensation for all services or functions the shareholder performs for the Corporation. The directors may increase or decrease the salaries from time to time, upon unanimous vote.

4. **Additional Shares.** The Corporation shall not, without consent of all of the shareholders, do any of the following: (a) issue additional shares of any class or any securities convertible into shares of any class; (b) merge or participate in a share exchange with any other Corporation; or (c) transfer all or substantially all of the assets of the Corporation for any consideration other than cash.

In the event the shareholders agree to issue additional shares or securities convertible into shares, then each of the shareholders shall have the right to purchase any such securities so offered at a future date in proportion to his then respective interest in the Corporation at the time of such offer.

5. **Transfer of Shares.** No shares shall be transferred in any manner or by any means except upon unanimous consent of the shareholders. If a proposed sale is not agreed to by unanimous consent, a shareholder may resign from his or her positions with the corporation and be bought out by the corporation as provided below.

6. **Buyout.** Upon the death, resignation, adjudication of incompetency, or bankruptcy by any shareholder, or the transfer, agreement to transfer, or attachment of any shares, the Corporation shall purchase all of the shares of the shareholder so affected at the value of shares described below. Payment by the corporation for such buyout shall be within thirty days of the determination of value and the transferring shareholder shall execute all documents necessary to transfer his or her shares.

7. **Value of Shares.** The parties agree that upon execution of this agreement the value of each share of stock is $_____. This value shall be reviewed and updated once each year and at any time that a sale of shares is contemplated. New value shall be set by a unanimous vote of the shareholders. If the shareholders cannot agree, then the corporation's accountant shall be asked to set a value. If any shareholder disagrees with the corporation's accountant's value, he or she may get the value of another accountant. If the two accountants cannot agree to an acceptable value, they shall choose a third accountant to set the final value.

8. **S Corporation Status.** If the Corporation is an S corporation and if it reasonably determines that any proposed transferee is not eligible as a shareholder of a Subchapter S Corporation or that such transfer would cause the Corporation to lose its qualification as a Subchapter S Corporation, then the Corporation may so notify the shareholder of that determination and thereby forbid the consummation of the transfer.

9. **Endorsement.** The certificates for shares of the Corporation shall be endorsed as follows: "The shares represented by this certificate are subject to and are transferable only on compliance with a Shareholders Agreement a copy of which is on file in the office of the Secretary of the Corporation."

10. **Formalities.** Whenever under this Agreement notice is required to be given, it shall be given in writing served in person or by certified or registered mail, return receipt requested, to the address of the shareholder listed in the stock ledger of the corporation, and it shall be deemed to have been given upon personal delivery or on the date notice is posted.

11. **Termination.** This Agreement shall terminate and all rights and obligations hereunder shall cease upon the happening of any one of the following events:

(a) The adjudication of the Corporation as bankrupt, the execution by it of any assignment for the benefit of creditors, or the appointment of a receiver for the Corporation.

(b) The voluntary or involuntary dissolution of the Corporation.

(c) By a written Agreement signed by all the shareholders to terminate this Agreement.

12. **Entire Agreement.** This Agreement embodies the entire representations, Agreements and conditions in relation to the subject matter hereof and no representations,

understandings or Agreements, oral or otherwise, in relation thereto exist between the parties except as herein expressly set forth. The Agreement may not be amended or terminated orally but only as expressly provided herein or by an instrument in writing duly executed by the parties hereto.

13. *Heirs and Assigns.* This Agreement and the various rights and obligations arising under it shall inure to the benefit of and be binding upon the parties hereto and their respective heirs, successors and assigns.

14. **Severability.** The invalidity or unenforceability of any term or provision of this Agreement or the non-application of such term or provision to any person or circumstance shall not impair or affect the remainder of this Agreement, and its application to other persons and circumstances and the remaining terms and provisions hereof shall not be invalidated but shall remain in full force and effect.

15. *Gender.* Whenever in this Agreement any pronoun is used in reference to any shareholder, purchaser or other person or entity, natural or otherwise, the singular shall include the plural, and the masculine shall include the feminine or the neuter, as required by context.

16. *Arbitration.* All disputes between shareholders or between the corporation and a shareholder shall be settled by arbitration and the parties hereto specifically waive they rights to bring action in any court, except to enforce an arbitration decision.

17. *Choice of Law.* This Agreement shall be governed by and construed in accordance with the laws of the State of _____.

IN WITNESS WHEREOF, the parties hereto have executed this Agreement the date and place first above mentioned.

_____ [Name of Corporation]

By: _____,
        President

_____ Shareholder

_____ Shareholder

_____ Shareholder

_____ Shareholder

Appendix

Sample, Filled-In Forms

This appendix contains filled-in sample forms that you may find useful for use in your own limited liability company.

When photocopying them, be sure to expand to 8.5"x11" so they will be accepted by the court and government agencies.

TABLE OF FORMS

TRANSMITTAL LETTER

To: Secretary of State
Corporation Division
State Capitol, Rm. 100
Libertyville, FL 33757

Re: Williams and Johnson, L.L.C

Enclosed is an original and ___1___ copies of Articles of Organization for the above-referenced LLC along with a check for $___125___ as follows:

$__125__ for filing fee
$__---__ for _____

Please send acknowledgement of receipt and/or date-stamped copy to:

Bill Williams
Williams and Johnson, L.L.C.
123 Liberty Street
Libertyville, FL 33757

ARTICLES OF ORGANIZATION FOR A LIMITED LIABILITY COMPANY

ARTICLE I - Name:

The name of the Limited Liability Company is:

Williams and Johnson, L.L.C

ARTICLE II - Purpose:

The purpose for which this limited liability company is organized is:

to engage in any and all lawful acts for which an L.L.C. may be formed.

ARTICLE III - Duration:

The period of duration for the Limited Liability Company shall be: perpetual

ARTICLE IV - Registered (or Statutory) Agent and Address:

The name and address of the initial registered (statutory) agent is:

Bill Willliams, 123 Liberty Street, Libertyville, FL 33757

ARTICLE V - Management:
(Check the appropriate box and complete the statement)

❑ The Limited Liability Company is to be managed by a manager or managers and the name(s) and address(es) of such manager(s) who is/are to serve as manager(s) is/are:

☒ The Limited Liability Company is to be managed by the members and the name(s) and address(es) of the managing members is/are:

Bill Willliams, 123 Liberty Street, Libertyville, FL 33757

John Johnson, 605 Galt Street, Libertyville, FL 33757

ARTICLE VI - Principal Place of Business

The initial principal place of business of the Limited Liability Company is:

123 Liberty Street, Libertyville, FL 33757

ARTICLE VII - Effective Date

The effective date of these articles is ☒ upon filing   ❑ on _____

ARTICLE VIII - Nonliability

The members and managers, if any, shall not be liable for any debts, obligations, or liabilities of the limited liability company.

ARTICLE IX - Miscellaneous

New members can be admitted to the company with full rights of membership upon the unanimous consent of the existing members.

IN WITNESS WHEREOF, the undersigned members executed these Articles of Organization this __22__ day of
__March_____, __2006____.

Bill Williams
_____
Member: Bill Williams   Address:
123 Liberty Street, Libertyville, FL 33757

John Johnson
_____
Member: John Johnson   Address:
605 Galt Street, Libertyville, FL 33757

_____
Member: Address:

_____
Member: Address:

Acceptance of Registered (Statutory) Agent

Having been named as registered agent and to accept service of process for the above stated limited liability company at the place designated in this certificate, I hereby accept the appointment as registered agent and agree to act
in this capacity. I further agree to comply with the provisions of all statutes relating to the proper and complete performance of my duties, and am familiar with and accept the obligations of my position as registered agent.

Bill Williams
_____
Agent: Bill Williams

| Form **SS-4**
(Rev. December 2001)
Department of the Treasury
Internal Revenue Service | **Application for Employer Identification Number**
(For use by employers, corporations, partnerships, trusts, estates, churches,
government agencies, Indian tribal entities, certain individuals, and others.)
· See separate instructions for each line.   · Keep a copy for your records. | EIN

OMB No. 1545-0003 |

1 Legal name of entity (or individual) for whom the EIN is being requested **Williams and Johnson, L.L.C.**	

2 Trade name of business (if different from name on line 1)	**3** Executor, trustee, "care of" name

4a Mailing address (room, apt., suite no. and street, or P.O. box) **123 Liberty Street**	**5a** Street address (if different) (Do not enter a P.O. box.)
4b City, state, and ZIP code **Libertyville, FL 33757**	**5b** City, state, and ZIP code

6 County and state where principal business is located **Liberty County, FL**	

7a Name of principal officer, general partner, grantor, owner, or trustor **Bill Williams**	**7b** SSN, ITIN, or EIN **123-45-6789**

8a **Type of entity** (check only one box)

☐ Sole proprietor (SSN) _____	☐ Estate (SSN of decedent) _____		
☐ Partnership	☐ Plan administrator (SSN) _____		
☐ Corporation (enter form number to be filed) · _____	☐ Trust (SSN of grantor) _____		
☐ Personal service corp.	☐ National Guard	☐ State/local government	
☐ Church or church-controlled organization	☐ Farmers' cooperative	☐ Federal government/military	
☐ Other nonprofit organization (specify) · _____	☐ REMIC	☐ Indian tribal governments/enterprises	
☒ Other (specify) · **LLC**	Group Exemption Number (GEN) · _____		

8b If a corporation, name the state or foreign country (if applicable) where incorporated | State _____ | Foreign country _____

9 **Reason for applying** (check only one box)

☒ Started new business (specify type) · _____ **clothing manufacturer**	☐ Banking purpose (specify purpose) · _____
	☐ Changed type of organization (specify new type) · _____
☐ Hired employees (Check the box and see line 12.)	☐ Purchased going business
☐ Compliance with IRS withholding regulations	☐ Created a trust (specify type) · _____
☐ Other (specify) ·	☐ Created a pension plan (specify type) · _____

10 Date business started or acquired (month, day, year) **10-07-2003**	**11** Closing month of accounting year **December**

12 First date wages or annuities were paid or will be paid (month, day, year). **Note:** *If applicant is a withholding agent, enter date income will first be paid to nonresident alien. (month, day, year)* . . . . · **10-22-2005**

13 Highest number of employees expected in the next 12 months. **Note:** *If the applicant does not expect to have any employees during the period, enter "-0-."*	Agricultural **0**	Household **0**	Other **2**

14 Check **one** box that best describes the principal activity of your business.

☐ Construction	☐ Rental & leasing	☐ Transportation & warehouse	☐ Health care & social assistance	☐ Wholesale–agent/broker
☐ Real estate	☒ Manufacturing	☐ Finance & insurance	☐ Accommodation & food service	☒ Wholesale–other ☒ Retail
			☐ Other (specify)	

15 Indicate principal line of merchandise sold; specific construction work done; products produced; or services provided.
clothing manufacturer

16a Has the applicant ever applied for an employer identification number for this or any other business? . . . . . ☐ Yes   ☐ No
Note: *If "Yes," please complete lines 16b and 16c.*

16b If you checked "Yes" on line 16a, give applicant's legal name and trade name shown on prior application if different from line 1 or 2 above.
Legal name · _____   Trade name · _____

16c Approximate date when, and city and state where, the application was filed. Enter previous employer identification number if known.

Approximate date when filed (mo., day, year)	City and state where filed	Previous EIN

Third Party Designee	Complete this section **only** if you want to authorize the named individual to receive the entity's EIN and answer questions about the completion of this form.	
	Designee's name	Designee's telephone number (include area code) ( )
	Address and ZIP code	Designee's fax number (include area code) ( )

Under penalties of perjury, I declare that I have examined this application, and to the best of my knowledge and belief, it is true, correct, and complete.

	Applicant's telephone number (include area code) **(518) 555-0000**
Name and title (type or print clearly) · **Bill Williams, Partner**	
Signature · *Bill Williams* Date · **10/15/2003**	Applicant's fax number (include area code) **(518) 555-0001**

For Privacy Act and Paperwork Reduction Act Notice, see separate instructions.   Cat. No. 16055N   Form **SS-4** (Rev. 12-2001)

Form **8832**
(Rev. September 2002)
Department of the Treasury
Internal Revenue Service

Entity Classification Election

OMB No. 1545-1516

Type or Print

Name of entity
Williams and Johnson, L.L.C.

EIN ▶ 59:12345678

Number, street, and room or suite no. If a P.O. box, see instructions.
123 Liberty Street

City or town, state, and ZIP code. If a foreign address, enter city, province or state, postal code and country.
Libertyville, FL 33757

1 Type of election (see instructions):

a ☒ Initial classification by a newly-formed entity.

b ☐ Change in current classification.

2 Form of entity (see instructions):

a ☐ A domestic eligible entity electing to be classified as an association taxable as a corporation.

b ☒ A domestic eligible entity electing to be classified as a partnership.

c ☐ A domestic eligible entity with a single owner electing to be disregarded as a separate entity.

d ☐ A foreign eligible entity electing to be classified as an association taxable as a corporation.

e ☐ A foreign eligible entity electing to be classified as a partnership.

f ☐ A foreign eligible entity with a single owner electing to be disregarded as a separate entity.

3 Disregarded entity information (see instructions):
a Name of owner ▶ ....
b Identifying number of owner ▶ ....
c Country of organization of entity electing to be disregarded (if foreign) ▶ ....

4 Election is to be effective beginning (month, day, year) (see instructions) . . . .▶ ___ / ___ / ___

5 Name and title of person whom the IRS may call for more information

Bill Williams

6 That person's telephone number

(909)555-1212

Consent Statement and Signature(s) (see instructions)

Under penalties of perjury, I (we) declare that I (we) consent to the election of the above-named entity to be classified as indicated above, and that I (we) have examined this consent statement, and to the best of my (our) knowledge and belief, it is true, correct, and complete. If I am an officer, manager, or member signing for all members of the entity, I further declare that I am authorized to execute this consent statement on their behalf.

Signature(s)	Date	Title
Bill Williams	*Oct. 15, 2005*	Member
John Johnson	*Oct. 15, 2005*	Member

For Paperwork Reduction Act Notice, see page 4.

Cat. No. 22598R

Form **8832** (Rev. 9-2002)

BILL OF SALE

The undersigned, in consideration of membership interest in _____ Galt Industries, L.L.C. _____

_____, a _____ Colorado _____ limited liability company, hereby grants, bar-

gains, sells, transfers, and delivers unto said corporation the following goods and chattels:

A 1997 Ford panel truck, VIN 1234567890 valued at $12,600
a G&R industrial lathe, Model 605 valued at $2,800

To have and to hold the same forever.

And the undersigned, their heirs, successors, and administrators, covenant and warrant that they are the lawful

owners of the said goods and chattels and that they are free from all encumbrances. That the undersigned have the

right to sell this property and that they will warrant and defend the sale of said property against the lawful claims

and demands of all persons.

IN WITNESS whereof the undersigned have executed this Bill of Sale this __1__ day of _____ May _____,

_2006_ .

_____ *John Galt* _____
John Galt

_____

_____

SCHEDULE A
TO LIMITED LIABILITY COMPANY
OPERATING OR MANAGEMENT AGREEMENT OF
Williams and Johnson, L.L.C.

1. Initial member(s): The initial member(s) are:

Bill Willliams, 123 Liberty Street, Libertyville, FL 33757

John Johnson, 605 Galt Street, Libertyville, FL 33757

2. Capital Contribution(s): The capital contribution(s) of the member(s) is/are:

Bill Willliams, $5,000 cash

John Johnson, $2,000 cash, 2002 GMC truck valued at $3,000

3. Profits and Losses: The profits, losses, and other tax matters shall be allocated among the members in the following percentages:

Bill Willliams, 50%

John Johnson, 50%

4. Management: The company shall be managed by:

Bill Willliams, 123 Liberty Street, Libertyville, FL 33757

John Johnson, 605 Galt Street, Libertyville, FL 33757

5. Registered Agent: The initial registered agent and registered office of the company are:

Bill Williams, 123 Liberty Street, Libertyville, FL 33757

John Johnson, 605 Galt Street, Libertyville, FL 33757

6. The tax matters partner is:

Bill Willliams

MINUTES OF A MEETING OF MEMBERS OF

Williams and Johnson, L.L.C.

A meeting of the members of the company was held on ___May 2, 2006___, at
___123 Liberty Street, Libertyville, FL 33757___.

The following were present, being all the members of the limited liability company:
___Bill Williams___   ___John Johnson___
_____   _____
_____   _____

The meeting was called to order and it was moved, seconded, and unanimously carried that
___Bill Williams___ act as Chairman and that ___John Johnson___ act as Secretary.

After discussion and upon motion duly made, seconded, and carried the following resolution(s) were
adopted:

The company agreed to buy a warehouse on Highway 31 in Libertyville and to finance
it it with a loan of $120,000 borrowed from Liberty Bank at 9% interest payable over 20
years.

There being no further business to come before the meeting, upon motion duly made, seconded, and unanimously carried, it was adjourned.

John Johnson
Secretary

Members:

Bill Williams

John Johnson

_____

_____

CERTIFICATE OF AUTHORITY
FOR
Williams and Johnson, L.L.C.

This is to certify that the above limited liability company is managed by its

☒ members

❑ managers

who are listed below and that each of them is authorized and empowered to transact business on behalf of the company.

Name

Address

Bill Williams

123 Liberty Street

Libertyville, FL 33757

John Johnson

605 Galt Street

Libertyville, FL 33757

Date: _____ May 29, 2006 _____

Name of company:

Williams and Johnson, L.L.C.

By: *Bill Williams*

Bill Williams

Position: Member

BANKING RESOLUTION OF

_____Williams and Johnson, L.L.C._____

The undersigned, being a member of the above limited liability company authorized to sigh this resolution, hereby certifies that on the __6__ day of ____June____, __2006__ the members of the limited liability company adopted the following resolution:

RESOLVED that the limited liability company open bank accounts with _Liberty Bank_____ and that the members of the company are authorized to take such action as is necessary to open such accounts; that the bank's printed form of resolution is hereby adopted and incorporated into these minutes by reference; and, that any __1__ of the following person(s) shall have signature authority over the account:

_____Bill Williams_____   _____John Johnson_____

_____   _____;

and, that said resolution has not been modified or rescinded.

Date: ____June 6, 2006_____

Bill Williams
_____
Authorized member

Index

employer identification number, 23,
54, 114, 129, 132
endorsement, 112
entire agreement, 113
equipment, 49, 53, 56, 91
estate planning, 14, 84
exclusive rights, 36, 102
expenses, 14, 20, 50, 85, 92, 93, 128,
148

F

fees, 4, 6, 15, 20, 26, 36, 37, 52, 71,
85, 90, 100, 102, 103, 106, 122,
129, 130, 131, 147, 148
fictitious name, 23, 32, 34, 37, 38,
54, 98, 100, 101, 122, 129, 132
filing documents, 38
financial statements, 71, 148
financially astute, 59, 135, 136
formalities, 11, 69, 70, 77, 87, 96,
112, 145
forms, 29, 37, 38, 39, 43, 50, 79,
100, 103, 106, 114, 122, 128,
129, 146
fraud, 58, 134

G

good faith, 147
goods, 34, 36, 101, 102, 122
class of, 36, 102

H

health and safety, 51
home business, 53

I

income, 3, 16, 20, 26, 27, 29, 50, 56,
60, 62, 71, 90, 91, 92, 93, 94,
122, 124, 136, 144, 148
industry code, 39
information return, 92
insurance, 15, 18, 27, 36, 42, 64, 65,
67, 68, 80, 81, 84, 85, 92, 93, 94,
102, 138, 139, 141, 142
Internal Revenue Code, 19, 87, 124
Internal Revenue Service (IRS), 3, 4,
26, 29, 50, 51, 54, 62, 81, 90, 92,
114, 128, 129, 132, 144
Internet, 33, 37, 38, 39, 61, 62, 98,
100, 106, 143
intrastate offering, 59, 136
investment, 10, 17, 57, 59, 60, 76,
80, 104, 107, 133, 134, 135, 136
initial, 10, 76, 80, 104
IRS Form 2553, 51, 54, 92, 114,
128, 129, 132
IRS Form 8832, 50, 51, 54
IRS Form 941, 50, 114
IRS Form SS-4, 50, 54, 114, 129,
132
IRS Form W-4, 50, 114

J

joint ownership, 124

About the Author

Mark Warda received his BA from the University of Illinois in Chicago and his JD from the University of Illinois in Champaign. He has written or co-authored more than seventy-five books, including *Incorporate in Florida* and *The Complete Nonprofit Corporation Kit*.